Exploring the Bible

FOUNDATIONS FOR LEARNING

EXPLORING
THE BIBLE

ERIC D. BARRETO and
MICHAEL J. CHAN

EXPLORING THE BIBLE

Cover design: Laurie Ingram
Interior design and typesetting: PerfecType, Nashville, TN

Library of Congress Cataloging-in-Publication Data is available
Print ISBN: 9781506401041
eBook ISBN: 9781506401058

The paper used in this publication meets the minimum requirements of American National Standard for Information Sciences — Permanence of Paper for Printed Library Materials, ANSI Z329.48-1984.

Manufactured in the U.S.A.

Contents

PART
1

What Is the Bible?

Chapter 1

Who Are We As Readers of the Bible?

We never read the Bible by ourselves. Even if you go on a long hike to the middle of nowhere and camp under the stars away from cell phone signals and the noises of the city, you are not alone when you read the Bible. Even if you are on a silent retreat in a monastic setting, you are not alone when you read the Bible. Even if you hide in a closet and shut the rest of the world away, you are not alone when you read the Bible.

No matter where you are, you are not reading the Bible by yourself because we always carry with us traditions and cultures and relationships and experiences that have shaped us. Some of that shaping we can recognize easily and understand. We are aware of some of the biases we carry, some of the prejudices that shape our reading of these ancient texts, even if we would prefer not to admit them. However, much of our molding as people and readers happens more subtly, entering our reading of the Bible in ways that might not be visible to us. There are assumptions we bear that we cannot identify, fear identifying, or incorrectly deem an advantage instead of an obstacle. To use biblical language, we always read as part of a "great cloud of witnesses" (Heb. 12:1) who accompany us at every turn of the page.

For instance, both of the authors of this book are men. And so it might be easier for us to relate to the patriarchs, disciples, and long list of male protagonists we find in the Bible. It takes the voices of women to help us notice the ways in which our reading practices prefer to notice male actions and voices but neglect to notice the absence of women's actions and voices, silence women's voices when they do appear, and diminish women's actions no matter how powerful. As Sandra M. Schneiders has explained, "Feminist interpretation also attempts to extract from the biblical text the 'secrets' about women that are buried beneath its androcentric surface, especially the hidden history of women, which has been largely obscured and distorted, if not erased altogether, by male control of the tradition."[1]

The story of Mary Magdalene demonstrates this reality rather well. Her name appears in all four Gospels. She is one of the faithful who witnesses Jesus' harrowing death on the cross (Matt. 27:56; Mark 15:40; Luke 24:10; John 19:25). She is there when Jesus is laid in the tomb (Matt. 27:61; Mark 15:47; Luke 24:10). She is one of the first witnesses of the resurrection, one of the first to discover a tomb now bereft of Jesus' body (Matt. 28:1; Mark 16:1; Luke 24:10; John 20:1). In John 20:11–18, she is the first public witness of the risen Jesus. In other words, these Gospel accounts agree that Mary Magdalene was a faithful follower of Jesus; she was a witness of his life, death, and resurrection. She was an exemplary disciple.

And yet what most of us "know" about Mary Magdalene is that she was a prostitute who gave up a sinful life to follow Jesus. Except that she wasn't a prostitute. Such "knowledge" has no backing in the Bible itself. Such flawed interpretations about who she was emerge from a misreading of the Gospel of Luke, a misreading imbued with certain assumptions about sinfulness and gender. Go back and read Luke 7:36–50 and 8:1–3. You will not find this well-worn assumption in those texts. "It is curious that although the text does not say what sort of sins the woman had committed, much attention has been given to speculation on the nature of her sinful past," Barbara E. Reid concludes.[2]

What does this all have to do with how we, your authors, read as men? Assumptions about sexuality and sinfulness and what is possible for these female followers of Jesus opened the way to flawed conclusions. These interpretations reveal more about us as interpreters than they do about the text. Too many powerful and influential men saw in Mary Magdalene a prostitute Jesus redeemed from her iniquity rather than a resourceful, faithful, and wealthy woman whose resilience and courage at the cross and tomb put male disciples to shame.

That is, we all suffer due to cultural and ideological blind spots. When we open the Bible, we have already predetermined what kinds of questions we want to ask and perhaps even the scope of responses we might receive in our reading. We have already assumed certain things about the people whose stories we read. And those assumptions too often are tinged with unexamined prejudices about gender, race, ethnicity, sexuality, and on down the list of various and contested forms of identity.

That is, were we not to examine our complex social locations as readers, we might too easily mistake our particular perspectives for universal truth, valid across all space and time. Unaware of our limited perspective and the ways in which our reading might inflict harm upon others, our interpretations might too easily effect oppression and diminish those among us who can least afford to be dismissed by God's word. The perspectives of others help to generate humility in us as readers, helping us to recognize that where we read from matters a great deal.

But that's not the whole story either.

Knowing who we are when we read the Bible is not just a matter of protecting ourselves from our worst biases. This acknowledgment of our locatedness, of the limitations of our particular perspectives, is also *good news*. Sometimes, even many times, our cultural location means we miss certain parts of the text or interpret it in ways that oppress others, but it is also true that our communities and our perspectives are vibrant locations of the Spirit's moving.

Our vision of Scripture may be narrow, even destructive, but it can also be rich and fruitful and liberating. You and your communities will see things that others will miss, and in that way your perspective can be a gift to your neighbor, revealing what was previously obscured to them and demonstrating new paths for following God's call.

For instance, Justo González writes about the parable of the laborers in Matt. 20:1–16 in a way that helped us see this text very differently. You might remember this story. In the parable, Jesus recounts how a landowner went out to hire workers at various times during the day. He hired some early in the day, others in the middle, and finally several even as the day was closing. When the work was done, the landowner paid first those who had started working the latest, those who worked the least. They were paid a day's wage. Those who worked all day believed that they would be rewarded in proportion to their labors. If someone worked but an hour and received a full day's wage, how much more should the worker who began earlier in the day expect? Their hopes were dashed when the landowner paid everyone equitably. Now, what does this story mean?

González explains, "When this story is read in most churches, there is a general reaction that the whole thing is unfair. It is just not right that people who worked more should be paid the same as people who worked less. In that social context, all that is seen is the injustice, and the sermon then usually argues that God's grace is above justice."[3] A very different interpretation of this text can be found in churches where people know something about the experience of waiting for hours on end in a market, yearning for any kind of work. For people who know the dejection of waiting and wanting and the hopefulness that comes with meaningful labor, this is not a story of injustice whatsoever. Instead, González notes, "The landowner's act in paying them a full day's wage is not a show of a grace that goes against justice, but rather of a grace that understands justice at a deeper level than is customary. The landowner pays them what they justly need and what they justly deserve, not what society, with its twisted understanding of justice, would pay them."[4]

This reading was transformative for one of the authors of this book in particular. One of us is Latino like González, but because I was born in Puerto Rico with US citizenship, my family never struggled with issues of immigration and its requisite documents in the same way our sisters and brothers from Mexico and Central America do. That is, though we as Latinas/os shared a particular cultural label, I could not see their plight and connect it to these stories. Having heard this transformative interpretation, I find that I think about this parable more often and in a richer way. Whenever I headed to my local Home Depot and saw a group of workers on a weekend, I would think about this parable. When I would return later that day because I was missing a part, as often happens when working on home improvement projects, I would see a smaller crowd of workers holding on to hope. And even late in the day, the hope of a few would still linger.

There, I saw a picture of the kingdom of God, a picture I could not see by myself but that my neighbor could help me see. And in opening my vision, my neighbor helped me see God more clearly. In helping me see God more clearly, my faith found a deeper resonance. In that deeper resonance was a profound sense of what God's justice might look like in our midst.

So also, you too can bring particular insight in your preaching and teaching and pastoral care. Knowing who you are as a reader of Scripture will unlock possibilities for ministry at the most unexpected times. You will see something in the Scriptures that others cannot, and in doing so the Spirit will move in their lives. After all, the Bible is not just a rulebook designed to direct our every step, and neither is it just a collection of interesting stories. The Bible meets us in the complexity and potency of our various social locations, draws us into conversation with one another. And in doing so, these stories, these works of poetry, these apocalypses open up a space of belonging and hope.

You are studying the Bible in seminary not just so you can know who Abraham was and identify the various dates of important events of the ancient world. You are studying the Bible in seminary because it is the living word of God, a living word that will surprise and delight us, confront and comfort us, alarm us and alleviate our deepest pains. This living word, however, cannot speak without your voice. And you cannot speak with the conviction God calls you to without knowing who you are. And you cannot speak with that conviction if those sitting to your left and to your right look and think and act just like you do.

In short, the solution to the inherent biases we carry is not to be rid of them entirely. Nor is it to try to mitigate or ignore them when we interpret the Bible. Instead, when we read the Bible, we ought to bring our full, authentic selves to a text that will affirm and challenge us, confirm and transform us, delight and concern us. There, God speaks, and we can hear in a new way.

In order to help you begin reflecting on the relationship between identity and interpretation, this book contains an in-depth inventory of questions (appendix A). While you will certainly learn something doing this exercise alone, it is best undertaken with companions. Doing so will not only help you appreciate how deeply your own reading of Scripture is shaped by your past but also how valuable it is to interact with readers who have very different histories.

Notes

1. Sandra M. Schneiders, *The Revelatory Text: Interpreting the New Testament as Sacred Scripture* (Collegeville, MN: The Liturgical Press, 1999), 185.

2. Barbara E. Reid, *Choosing the Better Part? Women in the Gospel of Luke* (Collegeville, MN: The Liturgical Press, 1996), 115. See also Greg Carey, *Sinners: Jesus and His Earliest Followers* (Waco, TX: Baylor University Press, 2009), 8–11.

3. Justo González, *Santa Biblia: The Bible through Hispanic Eyes* (Nashville, TN: Abingdon, 1996), 64.

4. Ibid., 65.

Chapter 2

How Does a Text Mean?

As experienced as you are with reading, it may appear to be a relatively simple exercise. In fact, you are probably giving very little thought to the extraordinary number of discrete neurological and cognitive processes you are engaging right now as you read these words!

We could oversimplify matters. We could say that your eyes are capturing words and sentences, which your brain pieces together in order to discover meaning and purpose. In other words, the meaning of any text can be found in between the letters and words and paragraphs on the page. Meaning is there. Sometimes we have to dig for it, but it's there. And so, to extend the metaphor, in seminary you learn a series of skills—skills that we might conceive of as tools for excavation. Various forms of criticism and bodies of knowledge are your spades, your shovels, your picks that allow you to unearth the meaning hiding beneath the words on the page. Your job as a reader is a bit like that of an archeologist. Your job is to brush aside the detritus of history and language so you can get to that meaning hiding behind all those perky words and cultural contexts.

But it's not that simple, is it?

Even with all the best tools, scholars and lay readers can disagree, and vehemently so, about the meaning of biblical texts. We also know that Christians who sought to be faithful to God and God's word have gotten things profoundly wrong. Christians in our recent past believed wholeheartedly that the conquest of the Americas and the subsequent decimation of its native populations was divinely ordained and free of the intertwined sins of greed, imperialism, and ethnocentric arrogance. Christians in our recent past knew for certain that the enslavement of Africans was part of the order of the world created and sanctified by Scripture; some were destined to be masters, others slaves, and the Bible was clear about it. Christians in our recent past believed wholeheartedly that the segregation of blacks and whites was a proper way to keep apart those peoples God never intended to join, and the Bible was clear about it. In every case, our Christian sisters and brothers were utterly convinced that the Bible spoke clearly about these questions, its meaning transparently obvious to anyone who could read the texts.

And yet Christians today now know that each and every one of these interpretations had nothing to do with the gospel of Jesus Christ. Each was a denial of the good news Jesus spoke and lived out. Each brought destruction and death in their wake. Each was an outgrowth of sinful oppression, not the Spirit's redemptive and liberative action.

To be sure, you and I are not immune to the sinful confidence that we have read the Scriptures correctly even as we trample upon our neighbors. It is virtually certain that you and I believe in interpretations of Scripture at which one day our ancestors in the faith will shake their heads. "How could they possibly have believed that?" they will say. And they will be right—tragically so.

The challenge for us is therefore not just *what* a text might mean but *how* a text and its interpreters discern how God is speaking today. How we interpret this text is as important as what we conclude the text is saying today.

So, if meaning can be so elusive and our efforts of interpretation so inhibited by our sinfulness, what does responsible, thoughtful, faithful interpretation of the biblical text look like today? How can we possibly muster the courage to make a claim on how Scripture is speaking today? How do we combine conviction and passion with humility and charity for others? All in all, how do these texts that we confess to be word of God mean something today?

These are questions of *hermeneutics*, which is a big word that tries to capture the complexities, artistry, and importance of the act of interpretation. Hermeneutics asks questions about meaning but also about readers seeking to construct meaning. What are the elements of hermeneutics?

First, hermeneutics leads us to consider our place as readers, something we have already invited you to do in the first chapter. To recap, we always and inevitably bring the depth and breadth of our experiences, biases, and commitments to every reading of Scripture. We cannot—and neither should we hope to—escape the constraints of our rootedness in a particular place, time, and culture. That rootedness, that particularity is a gift that God has given us. Yet it is vital that we develop the wisdom to identify our biases, to name them, to discern biases that enhance our reading of Scripture and those that lead us down destructive path, to challenge some biases, and to enhance the depth of our understanding of our experiences.

Second, we ought to consider the very language of the texts we read. How does language work, after all? After all, as Jacob D. Myers has noted, there is nothing about the letter b that requires that we pronounce the letter as a b.[1] There is nothing about that particular shape, that particular piece of typography that demands a particular pronunciation. Instead, we have reached a social agreement of sorts. We English speakers have all chosen to agree that the symbol b stands for a particular sound.[2] So also, we have agreed that the combination of various sounds and letters represent words with a particular semantic range. We have agreed that *bee* is an insect, but *be* is a verb that equates two things. Moreover, words don't mean one thing; they mean many different things depending on their literary and performative context.

For instance, think of a word like *port*. What comes to mind when you read that word? You might bring to mind an area where boats dock. You might bring to mind a particular kind of Portuguese wine. You might bring to mind the left side of a boat. You might bring to mind a path by which computers or networks communicate to one another. And of course, these are all correct definitions of the word *port*.

Words like these are polysemic. That is, they have many (poly-) meanings (-semic). Whenever we encounter such words in a piece of writing, we do not stop to sort through each of the possible meanings of the words. Instead, literary context helps us quickly determine whether an author is referring to a digital interface or a beverage. That is, the words that surround polysemic words matter. If you are reading about sailing, you might expect one meaning. If you are learning to be a bartender, you might expect another. It matters also who is speaking or writing these words. What do we expect from the author whom we are reading? It matters also who is reading or listening. Your particular experiences might make you aware of some meanings of "port" while occluding others.

And if individual words are polysemic, what happens when we align various polysemic words together? Certainly, context will provide some clarity. But we will still experience a sense of uncertainty about what a text might mean. This is why when you go to the library, you can spend all day reading article after article, book after book about any particular verse in the Bible.

Third, then, we are also drawn to wonder about the source of these differences in interpretation. Here, we are drawn to remember the Bible scholar's favorite word: context. Context is powerfully shaping. By context, we refer to the ancient histories, languages, cultures, and practices that helped give shape to the composition of these texts. Part of the task of interpretation then is listening carefully to these various and intersecting contexts in antiquity and taking them into account when we read the Bible. For instance, we might want to understand the manifold imperial forces that rose and fell in the history of Israel. How would living under any of these particular empires shape how Israelites understood their faith in God's promises? Or we might want to understand how gender was constructed and performed in various ancient contexts. What did it mean to be a woman or a man in the ancient world, and how do those assumptions differ from those operative for us today?

But when we speak about context, we are not just referring to the ancient world. We are not just contending that ancient texts need to be set in a particular context. We too are creatures of our contexts. We too are shaped powerfully by the histories, languages, cultures, and practices that inscribe our lives. That is, our contemporary contexts will shape profoundly what we read, how we read, and why we read.

For instance, we might draw a distinction between a hermeneutics of *trust* and a hermeneutics of *suspicion*. Some of us come to Scripture assuming we will find there words of life and affirmation. Our histories and cultures have taught us that these texts are on our side, so to speak, that they narrate a God who will sustain us through all trouble.

But such a stance or posture is simply not possible for some of us. Some of us have been the victims of distorted interpretations of these texts. Some of us have felt the sharp edge of these readings and had our basic humanity questioned under the guise of faithful interpretation. Indeed, some of us will find not just troubling *interpretations* but *texts* that are irretrievably against us.

Native Americans, for instance, might read the Exodus narratives not as moments of liberation of a people but the point at which one group was empowered to conquer the land of others, the Canaanites.[3] A hermeneutics of suspicion would wonder not just about the victors in a story but those whom God deemed extinguishable. African American readers might come to Scripture with a hermeneutics of suspicion.[4] After all, there were biblical texts that were used to resist Jim Crow even as other biblical texts were used to build and reinforce it. When a text can be drawn to such opposite conclusions, suspicion may be the best posture.

Women readers might also enter the reading of Scripture with a hermeneutics of suspicion.[5] The stories of violence perpetrated against women in the book of Judges and the sexualized portrait of the "whore of Babylon" in Revelation are striking instances of a text that speaks against the life and flourishing of women even as other texts (Miriam and Deborah and Mary and Phoebe) point in a different direction.

Shanell T. Smith captures this perspective poignantly, writing:

> "It loves me. It loves me not." This is the mantra I sometimes find myself reciting when I encounter the Bible, or people informed by its claims. Which phrase I utter depends on whether the text or its interpretations uplift, offend, or oppress me. Despite the subordinating rhetoric and violent imagery pervading the biblical text, or the negative experiences I encounter that result from an individual's or group's warped use of it, I cannot refrain from returning to its pages again and again—with a devout sentiment, no less. Some would say this is a form of insanity—my continual engagement with the biblical texts, while expecting different results each time. However, my expectation is based not on the notion that the abrasive and ruthless passages of the Bible would magically be rewritten before our next encounter, but rather on the prospect of new tools and ways of reading that can help to deal with these types of texts so that they do not cause further harm.[6]

Let's be clear: a hermeneutics of *suspicion* is not a stance that rejects faith. It is a stance that demands these texts and their interpreters be faithful to the God who inspires them and the people whose lives will be shaped by their reading. That is, these stances demand that our interpretations eschew oppression and reject cruelty. This hermeneutics calls us to be mindful of our mottled pasts, that we are not inheritors of an innocent history.[7] We too are embroiled in these troubling interpretive traditions and very well could remain within their grip. Even if you as an individual tend to read with a hermeneutics of trust, one that assumes that the texts of Scripture will speak *for* you and not *against* you, you still need and must heed those who read with a hermeneutics of suspicion. Theirs is a reading that will amplify the riches of Scripture and its troubling misinterpretations both yesterday and today.

So, what does a text mean? In the end, the paths we take to discern what these texts mean are as critical as our conclusions about meaning and significance. Attention to both is utterly necessary in faithful interpretation of Scripture. It matters whose voices we heed. It matters whose experiences we privilege. It matters whose interpretations we trust and whose we dismiss without much thought.

We have begun to explore the complexities of reading in this chapter. Contexts matter. Histories matter. Cultures matter. Peoples matter. All these matter in interpretation when we seek to proclaim some word of gospel about a God who has breathed life into us even as we have sought ways to stifle this vitalizing Spirit.

Texts mean by means of *encounter*. In the encounter of ancient texts and people today, of ancient empires and modern governments, of the powerful and the oppressed, of the educated and those who have honed wisdom in other ways, we discern alongside others how these texts speak into our communities today. As we noted earlier, we never read the Bible by ourselves. Perhaps we could add that we ought never try to interpret alone either, for the fuller possibilities of a biblical text can only be constructed in the fruitful and sometimes painful encounter of difference.

◯᙭◯ Notes

1. See Jacob D. Myers, "Reading Critically," in *Reading Theologically*, ed. Eric D. Barreto (Minneapolis, MN: Fortress Press, 2014), 75–94.

2. Though, of course, speakers of other languages may choose to agree that the sound that letter makes could be quite different.

3. Robert Warrior, "Canaanites, Cowboys, and Indians," *Christianity and Crisis* 49 (1989): 261–65.

4. There are a number of excellent collections of essay and commentaries by African American biblical interpreters that demonstrate well the diversity and unity of African American readings of Scripture. See, e.g., Cain Hope Felder, ed., *Stony the Road We Trod: African American Biblical Interpretation* (Minneapolis, MN: Fortress Press, 1991) and Brian K. Blount, ed., *True to Our Native Land: An African American New Testament Commentary* (Minneapolis, MN: Fortress Press, 2007).

5. See, e.g., Ilana Pardes, *Countertraditions in the Bible: A Feminist Approach* (Cambridge, MA: Harvard University Press, 1992) and Phyllis Trible, *Texts of Terror: Literary-Feminist Readings of Biblical Narratives* (Minneapolis, MN: Fortress Press, 1984).

6. Shanell T. Smith, *The Woman Babylon and the Marks of Empire: Reading Revelation with a Postcolonial Womanist Hermeneutics of Ambiveileince* (Minneapolis, MN: Fortress Press, 2014), 1.

7. See Justo González, *Mañana: Christian Theology from a Hispanic Perspective* (Nashville, TN: Abingdon, 1990), 75–87.

Chapter 3

Who Wrote the Bible?

So who wrote the Bible anyway? On the surface, this seems like a relatively straightforward question. After all, in the modern day, if we want to know an author's name, we simply turn to the title page, and we have our answer. Turn to the title page of any Bible, however, and you'll find publishers, translators, and publication dates—but no author.

As Christian theologians, we certainly want to affirm that God has been involved in the process of Scripture's creation. This claim takes seriously the fact that, at numerous points, particular biblical texts insist on God's involvement with the creation of Scripture: God gives the law to Moses at Sinai (Exodus 19–Numbers 10) and is the primary voice in prophetic books like Isaiah, Jeremiah, and Zechariah (see especially the phrase, "thus said the Lord"). In the New Testament, God gives a revelation to John (Rev. 1:1) and even visions to Paul (2 Cor. 12:1–10). Of course, in none of these texts is the Bible as a whole ever referenced.

The Bible never refers to itself.

The canons were established long after the biblical books were written. So even when texts seem to refer to Scripture (e.g., 2 Tim. 3:16), they have only a limited number of books in view, never the entire Bible as we have it. The result is that we as theologians are left to say something about the theological significance of the Bible as we have it, because the Bible does not—indeed, cannot—say anything about itself.

For a clue to these challenging questions, let's turn to one of Christianity's most important creeds, the Nicene Creed, and see how it talks about

Scripture's authorship. The clearest statement is this: "We believe in the Holy Spirit . . . *who has spoken* through the prophets." In these terse lines, the Nicene Creed offers a key insight: the Holy Spirit through the prophets and then the Scriptures utters God's words. Significant for us is the fact that Scripture is understood to be the product of *both* divine action and human action.

Embedded within the Nicene Creed is an important theological insight, namely that the God of Israel is a relational God, whose primary way of acting in the world is through creation itself.[1] In *The Bondage of the Will*, Martin Luther put it this way: God "does not work without us, because it is for this very thing he has recreated and preserves us, that he might work in us and we might cooperate with him. Thus it is through us that he preaches, shows mercy to the poor, comforts the afflicted."[2] God's decision to work through created agents is powerfully illustrated in Moses' call. God announces to Moses that Israel's cries have reached heaven and that God has come down "to rescue them from the hand of the Egyptians and to bring them up out of that land into a good and spacious land" (Exod. 3:8). But then, only two verses later, God says, "So now, go. I am sending you [Moses] to Pharaoh to bring my people the Israelites out of Egypt" (Exod. 3:10). So who rescued Israel out of Egypt? God? Moses? Well, both!

In the same way that God's own words and actions are hidden behind the words and actions of Moses, God hides behind the historical actions, motivations, and energies of the human authors and scribes who wrote Scripture. And throughout this process God makes no attempt to "rescue" the Bible from cultural influence. The Bible is, from beginning to end, a product of particular times and places.

What makes the Bible special—indeed, holy—is not that it provides an infallible accounting of historical events or even a scientifically reliable description of how the world was, is, and will be. Neither is the Bible in any way free of the limitations, frailties, and even sins of its authors and editors. What makes the Bible holy is that, as the church has preached, prayed, and read these texts throughout the centuries, it has consistently found itself addressed by God, in both judgment and salvation. When the church reads its precious texts, it so often finds that its texts also read the church, showing us how we are caught up in God's story.[3] Through use and interpretation, the church has discovered that when we return to the wells of Scripture, we consistently find there the manna we need in the wilderness.

The World of Scribes

In order to understand who wrote the Bible, we must understand something about how books were made in the ancient world. Texts from the biblical world clearly reflect different assumptions about authorship and textual production than those of the modern world. For instance, in the modern world authors and books are nearly inseparable. When a friend tells us that she has just finished reading an incredible new novel, we ask, "Who wrote it?" Or when we attend a book signing, we expect to meet the author, typically an individual. But very different perceptions of authorship and literary creation prevailed in the ancient Mediterranean world. For instance, it was very common for a text to be written or copied anonymously without any reference to the text's creator(s). As an example, the Gospels were all anonymously written, as were many Old Testament books (Genesis, Exodus, Leviticus, Numbers, Joshua–Kings, 1–2 Chronicles, etc.). In modern literary production, *anonymity is exceptional,* and named authors are the rule. The opposite tends to be true in antiquity.[4]

The primary producers of texts in the ancient world were scribes, who were generally charged with the following literary activities:

1. Transcription of oral lore
2. Invention of new texts
3. Compilation of existing lore, either oral or written
4. Expansion of inherited texts
5. Adaptation of existing texts for new audiences
6. Integration of individual texts into more comprehensive compositions[5]

The distinctions that one typically makes in the modern day between editors and authors were largely nonexistent in the ancient world. Scribes not only created literature, but they could also expand on texts, integrate them into larger literary compilations, and even transcribe oral texts into written literature. Biblical scholars often spend significant amounts of time searching for evidence of editorial changes, interventions, errors, and so on. And while results often vary from scholar to scholar, the underlying assumption that the biblical texts are marked by intense editorial activity is undisputed.[6]

Even though we are thousands of years removed from the scribes responsible for the Bible, we can still find evidence of their work. Some of the clearest examples of scribal activity are found in legal materials. Compare, for instance, the Passover legislation of Exodus with that of Deuteronomy.

According to Exod. 12:1–13, Passover should take place in a domestic setting. Turn to Deuteronomy, however, and one discovers that domestic observance of Passover is forbidden and that one must observe the Passover in Jerusalem alone: "You are not permitted to offer the Passover sacrifice within any of your towns that the LORD your God is giving you. But at the place that the LORD your God will choose as a dwelling for his name, only there shall you offer the Passover sacrifice, in the evening at sunset, the time of day when you departed from Egypt" (Deut. 16:5–6).

Behind these legislative changes, most biblical scholars detect the cultic reforms of Josiah, who, according to 2 Kings 23, reinstituted the Passover, which was kept "in Jerusalem" (2 Kgs. 23:21–23). Whatever the actual historical background, it is obvious that that these legal texts changed over time, and scribes are the responsible party—no doubt at the request of their royal patrons. Far from being a static reality, biblical law is often dynamic and responsive to new realities.

Scribal activity is also apparent in the first few chapters of Genesis. The Bible begins not with one creation account but with two originally independent texts that were interwoven at a later point by scribes. The two accounts are Gen. 1:1—2:3 and 2:4–25. Several pieces of evidence lend credence to this conclusion: (1) The name used for God in Gen. 1:1–2:3 is Elohim (typically translated "God"), whereas the divine name in Gen. 2:4–25 is Yhwh Elohim (typically translated "the Lord God"). (2) The sequence of creation is different when the two accounts are compared. For instance, the creation of animals precedes the creation of humans in Gen. 1:1–2:3, but in Gen. 2:4–25 humanity's creation precedes animal creation. (3) Related to point (2), in Gen 1:1–2:3, the first couple is created simultaneously (see 1:26–27), but in 2:4–25, the man is made first and the woman is made after the animals. All of this suggests to scholars that these chapters contain two separate accounts, which were at one time knit together by editors.

One interesting consequence of scribalism is that some books exist now in multiple versions. Take for example Daniel and Esther. The book of Daniel comes to us in two Greek versions (called Old Greek and Theodotian) and a Hebrew version that is represented by Codex Leningradensis, the medieval manuscript on which most English translations of the Hebrew Bible are based. The Greek versions are significantly longer than their Hebrew counterparts, and this is mainly because they contain additional material such as the Prayer of Azariah (embedded in Daniel 3), Bel and the Dragon, and Susanna. These additional materials are not found in the Protestant canon, but they are found in Catholic and Orthodox canons. What all of this means is that we can't really talk about *the* book of Daniel; instead, we have to talk about the *books* of Daniel.

The book of Esther also has a complicated scribal history. As it stands, the Hebrew version of Esther in Codex Leningradensis contains absolutely no references to God. The book is completely devoid of God-talk. The Greek versions of Esther, however, are full of references to God. For instance, after Mordechai and Esther learn of Haman's plot to destroy all of the Jews in the Persian kingdom, both pray to God for help.[7] The Greek version of Esther provides a completely different reading experience when compared to the Hebrew version of Esther. Like the book of Daniel, there is no book of Esther; there are only *books* of Esther. And Christians the world round call both "Holy Scripture."

Finally, Jeremiah 36 offers a unique example of how scribes may have partnered with prophets in the creation of biblical texts. The prophet Jeremiah lived during the last decades of the Davidic dynasty and in fact predicted its demise at the hands of the Babylonians in 586 BCE. According to chapter 36, one day Jeremiah received a word for the Judahite people (Jer. 36:1–3). This word was copied down by his scribe, Baruch (Jer. 36:4), who then read the scroll at the Jerusalem temple (Jer. 36:8–9). Jeremiah's words eventually reached the ears of the king (Jer. 36:16–21), who was so displeased with them that, every three to four lines, he would cut them off with a knife and throw them into the fire, "until the entire scroll was burned in the fire" (Jer. 36:23). After hearing about these events, Baruch and Jeremiah regrouped, and Baruch rewrote "all the words of the scroll that Jehoiakim king of Judah had burned in the fire." But Baruch didn't just copy the original message; he also added words (Jer. 36:32). Even though the narrative may be legendary, the scribal activities of Baruch reflect common scribal practices known from across the ancient Near East.

Human Word, Divine Word

Textual production in the world of ancient Israel was a complex and deeply human reality. At no point did God rescue scribes from their cultural and historical contexts. The full weight of their historical circumstances can be felt in the biblical texts. The Bible, like its authors, is incontrovertibly bound to the historical, cultural, and religious contexts out of which it grew. And God is somehow caught up in all of this mess, albeit in hidden and mysterious ways.

👀 Notes

1. See especially the theology of Terence Fretheim. See for instance his *God and World in the Old Testament: A Relational Theology of Creation* (Nashville, TN: Abingdon, 2005); Michael J. Chan and Brent A. Strawn, eds., with Terence E. Fretheim, *What Kind of God? Collected Essays of Terence E. Fretheim* (Winona Lake, IN: Eisenbrauns, 2015).

2. See LW 33:243.

3. Oswald Bayer, *Martin Luther's Theology: A Contemporary Interpretation*, trans. Thomas H. Trapp (Grand Rapids, MI: Eerdmans, 2003), 69.

4. Additionally, many important biblical texts (e.g., Daniel 7–12 and 1–2 Timothy) are even *pseudonymously* authored—that is, they are written by an anonymous author(s) who used the name of a (typically) revered figure from the past, presumably to endow the text with greater authority. For more information on authorship in the ancient Near East, see Karel Van Der Toorn, *Scribal Culture and the Making of the Hebrew Bible* (Cambridge, MA: Harvard University Press, 2007), 27–50.

5. Van der Toorn, *Scribal Culture*, 110.

6. Reinhard Müller, Juha Pakkala, and Bas ter Haar Romeny, *Evidence of Editing: Growth and Change of Texts in the Hebrew Bible* (Atlanta, GA: SBL, 2014).

7. A free digital translation of the two Greek versions of Esther can be found at http://ccat.sas.upenn.edu/nets/edition/17-esther-nets.pdf.

Chapter 4

Who Picked the Books of the Bible?

Were we to trust certain fictional accounts about the process that gave us the Bible as we know it, we would have to imagine a smoke-filled back room in the ancient world. Powerful people with devious agendas pick some texts for canonization and discard others into a roaring fire. Those texts chosen advance their narrow perspective as those that are burned pose a challenge to their hegemony. This is the conspiracy of conspiracies, a plan hatched long ago to keep the truth away from our eyes!

Such a narrative might make for fun summer reading by a pool. It is not good history. Worse, it betrays a deeply problematic theological vision of Scripture.

The sixty-six books that Protestants call the Bible or the seventy-three books that Roman Catholics call the Bible did not fall from the heavens one day fully and perfectly formed. These texts were not delivered by the angelic version of UPS complete with covers, a table of contents, and beautifully gilded edges. Instead, these texts were transmitted, written, shared, interpreted, digested, and reconfigured through generations of faithful followers of God. And while these faithful followers of God believed and confessed these texts to be the word of God, it took a long time for anyone to decide, "These texts are Scripture, but these others clearly are not." But at some point in time, we, the church, made these decisions. We, the church, chose some texts to function as Scripture, texts that we will read in worship and teach to new followers and ponder in devotion.

People made these decisions. And as we know, people are not always reliable. We are not always driven by the purest intentions. We can and do make mistakes aplenty. We can be seduced by power to believe in our own righteousness. It is also true, however, that we believe that God was moving in the composition and collection of the biblical texts. God inspired the Bible's many authors. God inspired those communities that together deliberated and prayed and discerned which texts spoke with the authority of God's voice. God continues to inspire us when we gather to read the Bible together and find in these words and the words of our sisters and brothers God's comfort and judgement, God's love and justice.

As we will discuss below, the precise historical shape of the process that eventuated in the biblical canon is still under scholarly dispute. What we hope you will see, however, is that a profoundly human process of canonization was also shaped by God's faithfulness. Our fingerprints are all over this process of canonization, but so are God's. God meets us in the messiness of a church trying to find its way in a complex and challenging world. One of the ways we found our way was in confessing that certain texts breathe living words of God when the faithful gather to interpret them.

Scripture and Canon

But first an important clarification. We often use the words *Scripture* and *canon* without precise definition. And in doing so, we make some category mistakes. *Scripture* is a text or texts that in our *practices* we treat as holy words of God. That is, we know some book is Scripture because we see a community drawing upon it in worship, individuals reading it in contemplative ways, and leaders calling it the word of God.

Canon requires yet a different layer of decision-making and practice. *Canon* means that communities look at *Scriptures* and determine that these are our texts but no others. Canon requires a closed list of texts, a list that can no longer be changed or adapted. Canon is a more formal, even final, decision about what counts as Scripture and what does not.

When we are looking for evidence of canon, these distinctions are important. We might, for instance, look to the early church mothers and fathers and see which texts they cite in their writings. Such citations will tell us that they viewed these texts as "Scripture," as words of God. However, it does not necessarily indicate that there was a clear, closed lists of texts from which they were working. Their citation of authoritative texts does not mean they had a Bible with set books. The canon might still have been open.

So also, we might find lists of texts in the first few centuries of the church. We might find a bound book containing texts from what we now call the New Testament. Or we might read Athanasius's letter to his churches in the year 367 CE. In this letter, Athanasius calls some texts Scripture, other texts he notes are helpful for new followers though they are not as full of insight as the first he lists, and other texts he excludes from the reading lives of the faithful. There is an important question to ask in both cases: Are these lists exclusive? That is, does the table of contents in the manuscript or Athanasius's letter exclude other texts entirely? Are the lists they write inviolable? Are these lists evidence of *Scripture* or of *canon*? And how much authority does any of these lists have over others?

And here is where scholarly debate becomes quite pronounced. Some scholars contend that the canon was closed sometime in the second century, while others see the text closing at some later point, perhaps in the fourth century.

While we don't have the room right now to help you settle these intractable questions, we want to invite you to consider the development of Scripture and canon as a theological challenge as much as it is a historical pursuit. That is, we are concerned not just with the *how* of the canon (who closed it and when?) but also with the *why* of the canon (why is the canon significant for those hoping to understand and proclaim the good news contained in its pages?).

To answer these critical theological questions, we need to set before us the processes by which the Old and New Testament canons came to be as well as what shape each Testament takes.

Hebrew Bible/Old Testament Canon

It is very difficult to speak with any certainty about the origins and processes that led to the creation of the Hebrew Bible canon.[1] While we know that post-exilic Jews were responsible for initiating these processes (Christians, of course, entered the canonization process much later), we do not know when, where, or how their work began. The evidence suggests that the canonical process was mostly unconscious, decentralized, and driven more by communal practices and customs than it was by a deliberate attempt to create a uniform and universal canon. Like we've said before, the story of the Bible is messy.

It is also important to recognize that the canonical process never resulted in a single canon. The order of the books of the Hebrew Bible used by modern Jews is different than the order used by Christians. The Jewish canon concludes with Chronicles and in particular Cyrus's decree that Jews may return to their homeland and rebuild the temple of YHWH (see 2 Chron. 36:22–23). The Christian Hebrew Bible canon, however, concludes with Malachi, which looks forward not to a restored temple but to the coming of Elijah "before the great and terrible day of the Lord comes" (Mal. 4:5 NRSV). For Protestant Christians and for Jews, the number of books is the same, but the order is different.

Some ancient sources refer ambiguously to early forms of the canon. For instance, the second century BCE Prologue to Sirach (a Deuterocanonical book) states: "Many great teachings have been given to us through the Law and the Prophets and the others that followed them, and for these we should praise Israel for instruction and wisdom."[2] What he means by the "others that followed them," however, is unclear and reinforces the claim that much about the canonical process is hidden. Jesus' statement in Luke 24:44 is similarly ambiguous: "These are my words that I spoke to you while I was still with you—that everything written about me in the law of Moses, the prophets, and the psalms must be fulfilled." While this verse may point to an early form of the tripartite canon (Law, Prophets, Writings), the status of the third part of the Jewish canon (the Writings) is unclear.[3]

Jesus and Paul never had Bibles. The Scriptures they had were loosely associated sacred texts, some of which made it into the canon of the Hebrew Bible that we know today and some of which didn't. We can begin to speak of a more well-defined canon near the end of the first century CE or beginning of the second century CE, and yet many questions remain. Apart from significant archaeological or textual discoveries, it is likely that the process of the canonization of the Hebrew Bible will remain obscure.

New Testament Canon

Like the development of the canon of the Hebrew Scriptures, the New Testament's canonization is a matter of controversy and uncertainty, though perhaps we can agree that the process was long, complicated, and not always easy to discern.

First, let's take a look at the shape of the canon as we have it. The New Testament is not arranged chronologically according to the date of the text's composition. First Thessalonians is perhaps the oldest text in the New Testament, but it is not listed first. Paul's letters were written prior to the Gospels, and yet the Gospels appear first in the New Testament. What then is the arrangement?

We might organize the New Testament around several categories. First are the four Gospels, narratives that describe the life and ministry, death and resurrection of Jesus. The book of Acts then forms a narrative bridge between the Gospels and the letters of Paul. In describing how God moved in the days of the early church after the ascension of Jesus, it provides narrative detail as a sequel to the Gospel of Luke. In addition, we tend to rely on Acts to provide an itinerary of Paul's journeys. After all, Paul did not leave his boarding passes tucked into his letters! Following Acts then are thirteen letters purported to be written by Paul. These letters are organized, generally speaking, from longest to shortest. After Paul's letters are a set of texts we often call the General Epistles or the Catholic Epistles. Though not all are letters technically speaking, some see a broader (and so "general" or "catholic") audience to these books than the particular cities to which Paul addresses his missives. We start with Hebrews, a text that looks more like a long homily than a proper letter. Following Hebrews is James, 1–2 Peter, 1–3 John, and Jude. The New Testament closes with the book of Revelation (notice that it's singular, not plural—Revelation not Revelations!), an apocalypse that resembles certain texts in the New Testament (Mark 13, for instance).

But how did we get these texts while others that some early Christians valued are mostly unknown to today's readers of the Bible? Why did the Shepard of Hermas or the Epistle to Barnabas or the Didache not find its way into the New Testament? What about those texts like Revelation and Hebrews that had a harder time than the Gospels or Paul's letters in finding their way into the canon?

It seems likely that several *sub-collections* emerged early on. That is, the four Gospels seem to have been grouped together as well as various collections of the letters of Paul. As early communities first received these texts, they must have shared them with other communities. At some point, the Gospels and collections of the letters of Paul started to travel together, so to speak. But the wider set of texts in the New Testament likely took quite a while to be drawn together; it might have taken several hundred years before someone or someones had the authority and power to close the canon, to declare some texts Scripture and others not.

Many scholars have argued that five basic criteria were used by these Christians to limit the scope of the canon.

Apostolicity: Did an apostle or someone closely linked to an apostle compose the text? For instance, the traditional view that the disciples Matthew and John composed their respective Gospels helped ensure that what they wrote was linked closely to the ministry of Jesus itself. But Luke and Mark, who were not disciples, could still be trusted because they were closely linked to Paul and Peter according to early traditions.

Orthodoxy: Did the text's theological teaching cohere with the emerging orthodoxy of the early church, or did it promulgate teachings contrary to that orthodoxy?

Antiquity: Was the text old, or was the ink still drying, so to speak? Older texts were thought to be more reliable because they were closer to the events they recorded and not as invested in distorting them.

Inspiration: Did the text show evidence of the Holy Spirit's inspiration? This fourth criterion would, of course, be closely related to the first three.

Usage: Was the text widely used by many churches and believers or only by a handful of followers in some regions? That is, a text that had received wide acclamation and use was more reliable than one preferred only by a few believers here and there.

And yet we might wonder how useful these categories might have been at the time. Do we imagine individuals and councils sitting around with checklists to decide a text's place in the canon? Or were these categories more loosely held? Were they basic parameters or strict criteria? Moreover, we might notice how interdependent these criteria were. For instance, we might notice how a text's inspiration and its orthodoxy might be two sides of the same coin.

So, how did someone or someones determine that some texts should be read as the word of God in worship, contemplated as sources of divine inspiration? Usage might be key here. Perhaps the eventual decision to canonize some books but not others was largely retrospective, a recognition of the usage and utility of certain books in geographically disparate places. Perhaps the canon was not a conspiracy to include and exclude so much as a recognition of what God had already done in the lives of various communities.

Does that mean that political intrigue, negotiations of power, and other less-than-theological motives were absent from this process? Of course not. The canon and the biblical text itself are rife with contestations of power. Yet we don't have to imagine a conspiratorial junta, a dark plot meant to silence some and empower others. We don't need a conspiracy—first because conspiracies are incredibly hard to maintain. It seems unlikely that such an exercise of power could sustain itself. But more importantly, we know that more ordinary exercises of power can be just as destructive and easier to execute than any secretive plot.

In the end, our canon comes to us covered in human fingerprints, both the best and worst of our efforts to discern God's voice. In that way, we find ourselves in much the same place that our ancestors in the faith found themselves.

Canon, Theology, and Christian Ministry

It is our conviction that a critical part of your vocation in ministry will involve reading and interpreting a particular body of texts. They might vary from tradition to tradition. We know too well that in many churches some texts within the official canons are consulted regularly while others are neglected habitually. A church might have an official canon and an unofficial but persuasive canon-within-a-canon. So what is the meaning of this closed, official list of texts?

At the very least, this particular set of books connects us to those who came before us in the faith. We share these texts with others who have struggled to make sense of faith in a confounding world. It was the same stories of Jesus that brought clarity and raised profound questions whether today or yesterday. It was the same stories of exile that brought hope and helped the faithful lament. It was the same stories of creation that brought promise and declared judgment on a good world gone awry.

The biblical canon also draws us to confront the diversity of Scripture's voices. The Bible canonizes diversity, deems distinct voices and perspectives the word of God. That is, the word of God is not univocal or homogeneous; the word of God is as vibrant and diverse as those who wrote, collected, and interpreted these texts. And so the task of the ministerial leader is to invite others into the diversity of voices with which God has spoken into this world. And in that activity of listening we may find ourselves hearing God's voice today in words we might never have expected.

 **Notes**

1. For an in-depth treatment, with an emphasis on primary sources, Lee Martin McDonald, *The Biblical Canon: Its Origin, Transmission, and Authority* (Grand Rapids, MI: Baker, 2007).

2. See ibid., 83.

3. For discussion of these texts and others, see ibid., 73–113.

Chapter 5

Why Does Translation Matter?

Most Christians read the Bible in translation, in large part because most of us cannot access the Bible in its original languages. Among the most popular English translations are the New International Version (NIV), New Revised Standard Version (NRSV), New American Standard Bible (NASB), King James Version (KJV), English Standard Version (ESV), New Living Translation (NLT), and so on. The practice of translating the Bible into English has a long and complex history. The first translation of the complete Bible into English was done by John Wycliffe in the late fourteenth century. Since then, numerous English translations have been made, with no end in sight.

But English was not the first language into which the biblical texts were translated. In fact, translation is an ancient practice that helps readers access literature written in less-accessible languages. The very first translation of biblical texts—called the Septuagint—aimed to do just this. According to one account (The Letter of Aristeas, second century BCE), a group of seventy-two scribes were summoned to Alexandria, Egypt in the third century BCE to translate the Pentateuch (Genesis–Deuteronomy) from Hebrew into Greek. While the Letter of Aristeas contains legendary elements, one can assume the broad contours of the event it describes: namely that in the third century a group of Jewish scholars translated the Torah from Hebrew into Greek in Alexandria. Eventually, all the books of the Hebrew Bible would be translated from their original languages

(Hebrew and Aramaic) into Greek. These Greek translations eventually became the Bible of the early church as we discussed in the previous chapter. Some modern-day churches (e.g., the Greek Orthodox) continue to read both testaments in Greek. From its beginning, then, the church has been formed by translations of the Bible.

Since translations are the primary means by which most Christians access biblical texts, it would be beneficial for us to reflect on the phenomenon of translation from an historical and theological perspective.

Reading in Translation: Advantages and Disadvantages

Every translation is an interpretation. Written language is made up of arbitrary signs (e.g., letters like a, b, c, d, e) which, when combined, make reference to ideas, things, actions, and so on. For example, in English, the combination of the letters d-o-g refer to a canine. There is, however, no natural connection between the signs d-o-g and the dog itself. The written script is arbitrary, but it has communicative value because English speakers enter into an unwritten agreement that the letters d-o-g refer to a canine.[1] A translator attempts to interpret the arbitrary signs of one language (e.g., Greek) and then to communicate her interpretation of those signs into another language (e.g., English). Since language is invariably embedded within particular cultures, discourses, and histories, one can never find a one-to-one correspondence between two words. There is no such thing as a "literal" translation. Every translation is also an act of interpretation. Translations, then, create both proximity and distance. They are, in the truest sense of the word, a literary re-presentation of a text through a secondary language.

Translation is also an exercise of power. Not merely literary achievements, translations have changed history and shaped the world we know, sometimes for good and sometimes for ill. The modern German language was deeply influenced by Martin Luther's translation of the Bible. According to one scholar, Luther's "Bible German" became the "ruling literary language within a century of its debut at the Wartburg castle, by the middle of the seventeenth century."[2] Similar language and history-shaping statements could be made of Jerome's translation of the Christian Bible into Latin or even the King James Version of the Bible.

One of the most fascinating examples of the intersection of translation, power, and justice is Clarence Jordan's *The Cotton Patch Gospel*. Let's listen to Jordan's own explanation of the project:

> While there have been many excellent translations of the Scriptures into modern English, they still have left us stranded in some faraway land in the long-distant past. We need to have the good news come to us not only in our own tongue but in our own time. . . . When Jesus told the story of "a certain man going down from Jerusalem to Jericho," every person in his audience may have felt as though he himself were that "certain man" who fell among thieves . . . but few of us would feel so personally involved. To give us a sense of participation or involvement, that "certain man" would need to be going from New York to Boston, or from Atlanta to Savannah, or from San Francisco to Los Angeles, or from our hometown to the next one. So the "cotton patch" version is an attempt to translate not only the words but the events. We change the setting from first-century Palestine to twentieth-century America . . . the Scriptures should be taken out of the classroom and stained-glass sanctuary and put out under God's skies where people are toiling and crying and wondering.[3]

Instead of finding 1 and 2 Corinthians, one finds "A Letter to the Christians in Atlanta" (1 Corinthians) and "The Second Letter to the Atlanta Christians" (2 Corinthians). Jordan's translation is vivid, justice-oriented, and often edgy in its attempt to give the New Testament modern flesh. It is a fascinating intersection of translation, power, and ethics.

Translations are clearly powerful. At their best, they can facilitate a meaningful encounter between the reading or hearing community and the text. But reading the Bible in translation also creates distance from the text. Reading the Bible in translation is like dating someone over Skype. To be sure, technologies like Skype enable you to get to know someone "face-to-face" at great distances. It makes possible previously impossible interactions. But even with Skype, you will never be able to visit your favorite park together, never be able to see a movie together, never be able to hold hands or share a meal. The medium (Skype) represents both possibilities *and* limitations. The same is true of translations. They give us access, but they also create distance.

Should I Learn Biblical Languages?

If you decide to attend seminary or your denomination's ministry training program, you may be faced with the option to learn biblical languages. Some programs require that you learn biblical languages, and some only suggest it. So should you learn them or not? Our answer: it depends.

We made the point earlier through several examples that the Spirit has been at work in the church through translations for millennia. Translations, in fact, have played an important role in the development of the church. Millions of readers have been given access to God's word because of these translations.

And yet, the fact remains that reading the Bible in its original languages provides us with a kind of proximity to the text that is not otherwise available. Close attention to the Bible in its original language allows us to gain greater appreciation for the literary artistry of the biblical texts. Many of the Bible's most cherished texts are profound, not only for their theological content but also for their literary artistry. Much of that artistry, however, is only visible if one can access the original languages. A few examples will illustrate the point.

Genesis 2:4–25 is a story familiar to many. It is a narrative in which God plants the famous Garden of Eden (Gen. 2:8) and creates the first human couple (Gen. 2:7–25) and the animals (Gen. 2:19). The literary artistry of this account, however, is only apparent upon close examination of the Hebrew text. Verse 7, for instance, says that "the LORD God formed man from the dust of the ground, and breathed into his nostrils the breath of life" (NRSV). The English translation, however, obscures an important word play between "the human" (*ha'adam*) and "the ground" (*ha'adamah*).

This is not the last time this story will use resonance to make a point. After failing to create a suitable partner for the first human from among the animals (Gen. 2:18–20), God tries again, only this time making a new creature from the first human's side (Gen. 2:21–22). In response to this new creation, the first human bursts into poetry:

This at last is bone of my bones
and flesh of my flesh;
this one shall be called Woman [*'ishah*],
for out of Man [*'ish*] this one was taken.

But in these examples, the author has more than just literary artistry in mind. Through euphony (words that sound pleasant in our ears), these words draw attention to significant relationships of mutuality and dependence. The first human (*'adam*) is derived from the ground (*'adamah*), demonstrating his dependence on the ground. And yet the ground's ability to produce plants is also dependent upon the human's working of the ground (2:5). The earth and the first human are existentially intertwined, and this relationship is subtly signaled by the rhyming of words. The same is true of the "Woman" (*'ishah*) and the "Man" (*'adam*). The woman and the man are in a relationship of mutuality and dependence. She is a "helper who corresponds to him" (Gen. 2:4 our translation). The term *helper*—often used to describe God and God's action (Pss. 20:2; 70:5; 89:19; 121:1–2; etc.)—is not derogatory but rather complementary. It points to the woman's power. The first couple complements one another. Derivation does not indicate subordination.

Another example of a play on words that seems impossible to translate in English can be found in Paul's short but powerful letter to Philemon. In verse 11, the NRSV translates, "Formerly [Onesimus] was useless to you, but now he is indeed useful both to you and to me." The key rhetoric in this verse is missing unless you can notice that the name "Onesimus" means "useful" in Greek. Here, Paul is using a word play in Greek to make a compelling case for how a master might see a slave in a new light. Utility takes a backseat to relationship. Usefulness is not nearly as important as the way God draws us together.

But there is one more striking piece of rhetoric one might miss if we only read the text in English. Paul begins the letter as he always does by listing both who is writing the letter in verse 1a but also who is being addressed in verses 1b and 2. Notice that the letter is addressed to Philemon but also to Apphia and Archippus (who are perhaps members of his immediate family) *and* the church that gathers in his house. This is a personal letter but also a communal communique. That this is so is evident in verse 4. In the opening of the letter, Paul is talking to a group of people. He lists them by name and uses the second person plural pronoun, a pronoun we don't "officially" have in English unless you are from the South, where y'all is used, or parts of the Northeast, where you might hear "yous." But in verse 4 and until verse 22, Paul speaks to Philemon in the second person *singular*. He is only talking to Philemon directly, and yet he draws upon the witness of the other addressees, the other witnesses to Paul's letter, to listen to this message as well. In both these cases, minor grammatical points reveal a very sophisticated rhetorical approach.

These are only a few examples among many in the Bible. Like modern authors, the ancient authors and editors of the Bible often delighted in probing the boundaries of language. The Bible is literature, and we need to read it as such. When we learn some Greek and/or Hebrew, we can better appreciate the Bible's literary dimensions and in turn more effectively interpret those texts in translation. Reading the Bible is just as much about studying human creativity as it is about studying theology.

So should you learn biblical languages? Again, it depends. It's our view that if you learn biblical languages and commit to using them in your study of the Bible, your efforts will be met with a richly rewarding experience, which in turn will be a blessing for those to whom you are ministering. And yet we also have known so many wise and faithful interpreters of the Bible who never attended seminary or learned biblical languages. Knowing Greek and Hebrew is no guarantee that we will read these texts more faithfully. They are useful tools for reading among many others.

Conclusion

Whether you choose to learn biblical languages or not, one thing is clear: God is at work in the church and in the world through the biblical texts, translated or untranslated. Translation can be seen as an act of faith that the God of Israel works through finite, historically particular means like language, literature, and translation, all for the sake of the world. This divine impulse to dwell among God's creation, even within finite realities, is fundamental to the God who enjoys an evening stroll in the garden (Gen. 3:8), who makes God's self available through the temple (Exodus 20–Numbers 10), and who finally takes on human flesh in Christ, only to die a human death.

⌾⌾ Notes

1. Onomatopoeia is one exception to this rule, since it attempts to mimic the natural sound, for instance, of an animal: cock-a-doodle-do, oink, or moo.

2. Eric W. Gritsch, "Luther as Bible Translator," *The Cambridge Companion to Martin Luther*, ed. Donald K. McKim (Cambridge, UK: Cambridge University Press, 2003), 71.

3. Clarence Jordan, *The Cotton Patch Gospel: Paul's Epistles* (reprint; Macon: Smyth and Helwys, 2004), xv–xvi.

Chapter 6

What Then Is the Word of God?

The last three chapters have sought to make one thing clear: the Bible, whatever else it may be, is a deeply human text. More library than book, the Bible emerged out of complex historical processes that involved politics, creativity, economics, and social realities. And yet, this profoundly human word is also God's word in two very important ways. (1) The Bibles we have in our hands today are a co-created text, its origins attributable just as much to humanity as they are to God. The Bible is both a divine word and a human word. (2) The texts of the Bible become God's Word for us when we interpret Scripture and most especially when Scripture interprets us.

Scripture as God's Work through Human Hands

To say that the Bible is God's word is to say that it is a *co-created text*, fashioned and formed by both divine and human hands. The Bible is a divine work, and the Bible is a human work. God's work in the creation of Scripture is hidden behind the everyday actions of scribes, poets, kings, and storytellers. Did they know they were communicating divine words? Sometimes. And sometimes not. Whatever the case may be, God was involved in the messy process of Scripture's creation.

It is very tempting to try to divide up the "divine parts" of Scripture from the "human parts" of Scripture. Some, for instance, might claim that beneath the culturally specific statements of Scripture are eternal truths that can be discerned. These truths, it is claimed, are God's true words, whereas the culturally particular elements are dismissible window dressing. But this attempt to separate the wheat from the chaff, as it were, is misguided and fails to recognize that Scripture, like Christ himself, comes to us embodied and time-bound.

We take a slightly different approach. We argue that Holy Scripture is the fruit of a divine *partnership* between God and humans. Humans were coworkers with the Spirit in the long process of Scripture's production. God didn't step in to protect the process from human hands but in fact allowed the variety of texts and Bibles to emerge in response to history, human creativity, and community practice. Instead of trying to liberate the Bible from its context (an impossible task, in fact) then, we urge you to embrace the fact that the Scriptures are situated, contextual, and grounded.

But this argument isn't simply an attempt to wed critical ways of thinking about the Bible to theological convictions about Scripture's holy status. Rather, our thinking about this issue emerges out of a particular *theology of divine action*. This phrase is just an academic way of talking about how God gets things done in the world. God gets things done in the world in many different ways. On rare occasions, God acts alone (e.g., Jesus' resurrection; Rom. 6:4; 1 Cor. 15:15), but more often than not, God acts in partnership with creation and especially human creatures.

The reformer Martin Luther made a similar point in his famous essay, *Bondage of the Will*. There he insists that God "does not work in us without us, because it is for this he has created and preserved us, that he might work in us and we might cooperate with him, whether outside his Kingdom through his general omnipotence, or inside his Kingdom by the special virtue of his Spirit."[1]

A number of biblical texts illustrate God's partnership with creation in a whole range of deeds, from redemption to judgment. Exodus 3 is particularly illustrative. In verses 7 and 8, God approaches Moses with this declaration:

> I have observed the misery of my people who are in Egypt; I have heard their cry on account of their taskmasters. Indeed, I know their sufferings, and I have come down to deliver them from the Egyptians, and to bring them up out of that land to a good and broad land, a land flowing with milk and honey,

to the country of the Canaanites, the Hittites, the Amorites, the Perizzites, the Hivites, and the Jebusites."

God resolves to free Israel from Egypt. But how exactly God will accomplish this isn't revealed until verse 9: "So come, I will send you [Moses] to Pharaoh to bring my people, the Israelites, out of Egypt." So who actually freed Israel from Egypt? God? Moses? Yes, both.

God often judged Israel by means of foreign rulers. Isaiah 10:5–7, for instance, describes a time when Assyria, an ancient Mesopotamian power, was called upon by God to bring judgment against Israel:

Ah, Assyria, the rod of my anger—
    the club in their hands is my fury!
Against a godless nation I send him,
    and against the people of my wrath I command him,
to take spoil and seize plunder,
    and to tread them down like the mire of the streets.
But this is not what he intends,
    nor does he have this in mind;
but it is in his heart to destroy,
    and to cut off nations not a few.

Assyria is here described as a tool in the hand of God. But the metaphor breaks down slightly when one realizes that this tool has more agency than one would expect from a mere tool. Assyria's intentions go beyond God's will; Assyria wants to engage in unsanctioned violence. As a result, God will judge Assyria too, alongside Judah (see 10:8–19, 24–34). The implication is clear: God's decision to use agents, while effective at times, comes with risks. Humanity has the ability to choose against God's will and intention.

Many other texts could be named.[2] Our argument is that in the same way that God used human agents to both free and judge Israel, God used human agents in the long history of the Bible's composition. The Bible, in other words, results from a partnership between humanity and God, who hides behind the deeply human activities of scribes, sages, and poets.

Because the Bible is the result of divinely inspired human agency, it is entirely appropriate for us to interpret it with an eye toward human creativity, artistry, and beauty. The Bible is literature, and often good literature. As such, we should feel free to bring the full range of literary and textual analyses to the Bible without hesitation or fear that in doing so we will denigrate the Bible's status as sacred literature. We misunderstand the Bible if we think that interpretation involves finding the right "balance" between its sacred and human aspects. Rather, truly honoring the Bible as a word of God requires us to read it as the result of human energy and creativity. Is the Bible a divine word, or is it a human word? Yes, both.

Scripture as Address

Finally, to say that Scripture is the word of God is to say that the Triune God (Father, Son, and Holy Spirit) addresses the world through the interpretation of these holy texts. The Bible by itself is simply a collection of ancient texts. Alone, the Bible does nothing, says nothing, and has no agency. It is only through the power of the Holy Spirit, at work in the processes of human interpretation, that Scripture *becomes* an address from God in time and place and for particular people. God's word is a particular word. That word brings us into an encounter with God, our neighbor, creation, and ourselves, often in surprising ways.

Scripture, moreover, is not only interpreted by us; it also *interprets* us. We are interpreted in those moments when we find ourselves in Scripture's stories, addressed by its concerns, created anew by its promises, wounded by its power, exposed by its demands, and inspired to love by its content. Scripture interprets us when we realize "that these stories talk about me; they tell my story."[3] Interpreting the Bible and being interpreted by the Bible are not options. The latter, in fact, cannot exist without the former. And it is to this intersection of anthropology and theology that the Spirit invites us. The moment of address when Scripture becomes the word of God is a moment of freedom, terror, joy, and release, when the creature is recognized by her Creator.

Interpretation is hard work. It takes effort and struggle. Forget not the lesson of Jacob, who received his word of blessing after an entire night of conflict (Gen. 32:22–32) or the Canaanite woman who only received Christ's word of healing after a verbal row with the Son of God (Matt. 15:21–28). These words came but only after long, tiring, and epic struggle. Suffering and interpretation are spiritual siblings.

The Bible isn't holy because it is untouched by the world or because it is free of human influence. It is holy because through it we encounter the Holy One, who is overflowing with grace and truth.

◎○ Notes

1. *LW* 32:243.

2. For a fuller discussion of texts like the two above, we direct you to the work of Terence Fretheim (see bibliography).

3. Oswald Bayer, *Martin Luther's Theology: A Contemporary Interpretation* (Grand Rapids, MI: Eerdmans, 2008), 69.

Chapter 7

Who Are We When We Read the Bible?

The Bible is a risky book to take up and read precisely because the Bible will change you. In God's voicing of and acting in love and justice, in the narration of God's faithfulness and human cruelty, in the poetic drawing of wisdom and foolishness, our reading of the Bible will shape an imagination for what the world is and what it could be. The word of God can help clarify our vision so that we can discern the injustice of the present as well as the ways in which the reign of God is already intruding into a broken world. The word of God will help us imagine a vibrant and just present with a future horizon marked by God's promise.

But such reading is dangerous because it might lead and inspire you to act in ways that put you at odds with the forces of various "-isms" that crowd our lives today. In a world infiltrated by the sinful notion of racism, you might dare to proclaim that God revels in our differences and rages against discrimination. In a world ruled by force, Jesus' condemnation of violence might place you on the side of the powerless. In a world dominated by avarice, you might dare to suggest that our possessions do not define our worth. Such readings are dangerous because they might call you to act like a prophet, condemning those forces that others think are inherent and ordinary. Such a reading is dangerous because it might dare you to hope in a God whose love seems distant, absent, and mythical but is actually present and tangible and transformative.

So before we turn to various texts of Scripture and the different ways they describe the world and imagine a new world in part 2 of this book, let's return to us, the readers of Scripture, and to the God who empowers, enlightens, and illuminates the paths of our understanding.

The "us" in that last sentence and the "we" in the title of this chapter are important, for the reading of Scripture is an activity of identity and community building. That is, whenever we read the texts of Scripture, when we read the word of God alongside other people, we confess an identity before the God of the universe. And not only are individuals shaped and formed by reading Scripture, but so are whole communities. Imagine a community in which the Bible provides a framework for being and belonging, an imagination for what life together might look like. That is among the most important calls you will have in leading a community of faith.

And yet the Bible has not always tended to function in this particular way in communities. In some communities, the Bible is a rulebook, a yardstick that determines insiders and outsiders, who belongs and who does not. In others, believers have not felt equipped to deal with the diversity of the Bible's voices, or they have been so burned by prior experiences that they would rather not read these texts. Between the misuse of the Bible as a communal litmus test and its neglect, there is space for an imaginative, grace-filled, community-forming way of reading Scripture. Your study of Scripture in seminary can help you learn what that space might be like and how a community might form around these practices.

This is who we might be when we read the Bible. Much could be said about this kind of biblical reading, this approach to listening to God's voice, but we might start with four critical starting points.

1. We listen to God's voice in the voices of our neighbors

As we argued earlier, we do not read the Bible by ourselves. Indeed, we need one another to notice what we don't notice when we read these rich texts. And my peculiar optic is needed by those around me. That is, we need one another to read these texts, for God will speak with and through the witness of our neighbors. I find that we often assume that inspiration was a divine activity of the past, something God did *then* when the texts of Scripture were composed and collected. But what if we open our imagination to an inspiration that is still with us, for a Spirit that still intercedes as we read and opens the text up as the Spirit speaks with and through our neighbors?

What if the ways God might use these texts to shape us and our communities are as inexhaustible as God's grace?

2. We listen to God in the witness of the oppressed and the vulnerable

Among our neighbors, we ought to heed the witness of those the world treads upon most, those among us who suffer affliction at the hands of the powerful, those whose voices most of us deem unworthy of our attention. Scripture records so many stories of God choosing unlikely and easily dismissed spokespersons that these choices reflect something of God's character. From Abraham to Moses, Miriam to Mary, Hannah to Anna, God speaks through the oppressed and afflicted, the neglected and marginalized who have not been forgotten by God.

The implications for this divine pattern are manifold for us today. What if God is speaking most powerfully in those communities we would prefer to ignore? What if God is speaking through a Canaanite woman in desperate need of the healing of her daughter or an Ethiopian eunuch on a wilderness road or the owner of a brothel sheltering Joshua's soldiers? What if God today speaks through those whose credentials we would scoff at, those whose education we deem insufficient? What if God today speaks through those who protest their mistreatment at the hands of a justice system most of us assume is on "our" side? What if the oppressed say something that we think cannot be true but is actually the very breath of God? We ought to listen because God has constantly surprised us with the unlikeliest voice teaching us that which God most wants us to hear.

Again, we do not read Scripture by ourselves, but especially we cannot read Scripture apart from the cries and hopes of those the world has trampled but God lifts up.

3. We listen to God's voice when we read the Bible between humility and conviction

Reading the Bible poses many challenges, and we may occasionally feel paralyzed before those challenges. How can we read the biblical texts with passion and conviction without at the same time making the Bible a weapon against others? We might also wonder whether we know enough about the ancient world to translate these ancient texts into modern contexts. We might wonder whether we can wield any authority in interpreting this text in front of a community seeking solace and salvation in a broken world. The tasks of interpretation and proclamation might seem too great when so many brilliant interpreters have gone before us, when the wisdom of faithful lay people demonstrates a depth of insight no seminary degree can guarantee. At other points, we might be so convinced by an argument that no other conclusion seems possible. What else could this text mean but this evident, indisputable conclusion? This is the answer to our questions, if only others would listen!

Both impulses are understandable. You will learn much in the coming years about Scripture, let alone how that knowledge and wisdom will mature in years of faithful ministry. Your voice and leadership will be vital in the communities you serve, and you are called by God to speak boldly and prophetically in these places. Yet it is also true that you will be stopped short by an insight from a lay person who never went to seminary or a question a child might ask. Despite all your expertise, you won't have all the answers. You won't and can't be the sole authoritative interpreter of Scripture in the communities you lead. And you may find that truth all too overwhelming. You may find that your confidence falters at all the scholarship that you have not yet read or the wisdom that one can only acquire after a lifetime of struggle and faithful witness or the unrestrained curiosity of the young. But in the end, such postures are insufficient to the call God has placed on your life but also the depth and breadth of the knowledge and expertise you will hone in the coming years. After all, an important part of knowledge is understanding its limits and trusting that God's Spirit has been faithful in your learning.

And so we might find ourselves at an irresolvable but fecund tension. We bring to our reading of God's word the convictions that God speaks through these texts and those who read them, that God is faithful to God's promises even if we have failed so often to live them out, that hope is never unavailing. We also come to the Bible with convictions about its meaning and significance for us and for others. We might even have strong opinions about the best way to render this or that Greek phrase. But all these convictions ought also be grounded in an equally passionate sense of humility. We know the limits of our knowledge, both scholarly and personal. We know we might be wrong, tragically wrong, about how we read these texts. We know that we will look back to beliefs we hold today and wonder in the coming years why we ever held such views.

And so we pose our readings between conviction and humility, certainty and expectation, hope and doubt. This is the very essence of faith.

4. We listen to God's voice by imagining the walls of our community ever widening, even dissipating

Last, this tension of humility and conviction ought to make us ready to expect that God will regularly, even shockingly, shatter the walls of belonging we construct. These widening horizons are not the product of our "evolution" into ever more inclusive people, and neither are they an indictment of our ancestors for not seeing what is so obvious now to us. Instead, this is a credit to God's grace. As Martin Luther King Jr. prophetically observed, "The arc of the moral universe is long, but it bends towards justice."

The Bible recounts a God of surprising inclusion and love. For instance, Acts 2 recounts the story of Pentecost, a miraculous moment of unity. The disciples are gathered together waiting for the promise Jesus had made them prior to his ascension. Jesus had promised them an extravagant gift, and the gift arrives in grand style. Tongues as of fire rain down from the heavens, and all of a sudden ordinary Galileans can speak every language of the world. The crowds gathered in Jerusalem are composed of Jews from every corner of the Roman Empire and the world. And yet they all hear the good news preached in their own languages. No matter where they were from, they hear the words that most speak to their hearts. The stunned crowd wonders aloud, "What does this mean?"

Too often, we assume that the meaning of this scene is the cessation of difference, the overcoming of our linguistic divisions. To many, this scene is a dramatic reversal of the Tower of Babel (Genesis 11), that moment when God afflicts the world with different languages, punishes human arrogance by creating the stumbling block of differences around our various places of belonging. This is a profound misreading of the Pentecost story, let alone the Babel story.

Why? If Pentecost were a reversal of Babel, if Pentecost undid that which Babel wrought, what should have happened when the disciples were imbued with the power of the Holy Spirit? They should have all spoken the same language! They should have spoken the language of the inhabitants of

Babel, or they could have spoken some perfect divine language with ideal syntax and precise vocabulary. Neither of these things happens. Instead, the Spirit learns our many languages and all their odd syntax and peculiar vocabularies. God does not ask us to learn God's language; God learns our very many languages. And in this way, we catch a glimpse of God's hopes for us: not that we would all become the same but that God's love would wrap us all up into God's family. Our languages and cultures would not be an obstacle to relationship with God and one another but a most valuable place where such relationship can take place.

God likes that we are different. God wants us to be different. God did not punish a proud people at Babel with the curse of many languages. Instead, God drew a scared people to fill the earth with the melodious sounds of different languages, the lovely odor of different foods, the power of distinct cultures and perspectives. And God does one more thing. God meets us in the midst of our differences and says that our differences are good.

Equipped with that kind of imagination, communities of faith today might be transformed into places of hopeful belonging. Churches may no longer see demographic changes in their communities as problems they need to solve or obstacles on the way to becoming the church God wants us to be. Those changes are where God already is, where God is already acting! Those are the places where God is calling us to be church.

The Bible is a risky book. It has been misused by many, manipulated to exclude or demean some and vaporize others. The Bible has also inspired many to call us to the kind of reign God designed. When we read this text, we risk duplicating the mistake every generation makes: assuming the texts of Scripture affirm us at every point without accounting for the judgment these texts contain. We also risk that when we read with others, we will have to account for this judgment, this divine declaration that repentance and reconciliation go hand in hand.

Who are we when read the Bible? We are those who hope and those who doubt. We are those who yearn and those who faint. We are those who seek and those who have resigned. Who are we when we read the Bible? We are the extraordinary creatures God has created while we are also the broken vessels God is seeking to restore.

PART

2

How Then Do We Read
the Bible?

Chapter 8

How Do We Read Creation Texts?

Introduction

The Bible begins and ends with creation (Gen. 1:1–2:24; Rev. 21:1–8). This means that God's work in making and remaking the world frames all of Scripture. With some justification, Christians have tended to emphasize God's work in salvation, but the Bible's literary structures suggest that Christians' emphasis on redemption alone has often come at the cost of ignoring the Bible's broader creational framing. Far from being in contradiction to one another, creation and redemption are closely related. In fact, one can say that salvation in its fullness is nothing less than the full, unveiled expression of God's promises to all creation.

But the interpretation of creational texts is not at all straightforward. This is an important starting place, not only because of the important place of creation in the Bible and Christian theology but also because of the prominent place given to creation texts in American public discourse, at least by some. Not a small number of Americans are engaged in a vigorous conversation about the role of creation texts in public spaces like school curricula and public policy. This conversation is often billed as a battle of science versus Scripture. Even if you don't participate in this debate, it is likely that, as a Christian leader, you will encounter it in some form or another, making it all the more necessary for you to spend time reflecting on creational texts. Ultimately, we'll argue that, for Christians, both scientific inquiry and the study of Scripture are crucial for understanding God, the world, and ourselves.

The first thing to note is that the Bible has many creation "accounts." The one most familiar to Christians is Gen. 1:1–2:3, which narrates the creation of the world in seven days. Other accounts include Gen. 2:4–25, Psalm 104, Job 38–41, Prov. 8:22–31, and John 1:1–3. These alternative accounts cannot be harmonized into a single, master narrative, at least not without doing significant damage to the integrity of the individual texts. Nor should one even try to harmonize them. Attempts to harmonize diverse texts often bear witness to a deep, unacknowledged anxiety about theological difference. How can God be God if God's word speaks in so many ways? How can Scripture, on the one hand, be holy and on the other hand be polyphonous?

As theologians, we do our best work when we are honest with ourselves and about our sources, acknowledging that the Bible contains several (sometimes contradictory) accounts of creation, and that the editors of the Hebrew Bible felt no need to harmonize these accounts into a single, seamless narrative. Each of these voices has a place in the canon, and to affirm as much calls neither God's character nor the power of God's word into question.

Next, it is crucial to realize that not all texts are true in the same way: *truth is relative to genre.*[1] The parable of the prodigal son (Luke 15:11–32) is one of Jesus' most potent parables. It speaks powerfully about human wandering, God's reckless love, and the human capacity to resent God's grace toward a sinner. But this parable's truthfulness is not dependent upon whether in first-century Palestine there was an actual father with two sons or whether one of those sons actually and historically squandered his share of the property. The story can be true without being historical. In order to appreciate how this story communicates truth, one must understand what the text can and cannot do for us, what questions it is actually trying to address. And the same is true of creation texts. Their truthfulness is not dependent upon their historicity or even their agreement with scientific accountings of creation. The Bible's creation accounts are asking fundamentally different questions than modern science. Both attempts to talk about creation are complementary, not contradictory. Charles Darwin, it turns out, may have been one of modernity's greatest gifts to the church. In the words of Mark Throntveit and Alan Padgett, "Darwin can also be a friend to biblical Christianity because he helps us look at the text itself through specifically theological eyes, helping to liberate the Scriptures from a narrow biblicism or a fixed dogmatic tradition."[2]

So instead of beginning with the assumption that the Bible's creation texts are trying to answer our questions about the scientific origins of the cosmos, begin with questions like these. How is this text true? What questions or problems is this text trying to address in the time of its composition? To what fears and anxieties is this text trying to respond? Is Gen 1:1–2:3, for instance, really trying to do the same thing that, say, Stephen Hawking's *A Brief History of Time* is attempting?[3] Or is the author of Psalm 104 to be understood as an ancient cosmologist, attempting to provide a scientific accounting of the origins of the cosmos? When in Job 38:4 God says, "Where were you when I laid the foundation of the earth?", are we to take this claim as a scientific description of how God fashioned the cosmos and argue that the cosmos is quite literally a building or a temple?

It is the task of careful readers to determine how these texts are true for us today, what they can tell us about God, the world, and ourselves. Before we approach the biblical texts with our modern questions, however, we should first make an attempt to understand and appreciate the questions and problems the texts are trying to answer, in their own place and time. One can never determine these things with certainty, but the exercise is nonetheless valuable, in that it often reveals how a text's interests might differ from our own and often in very significant ways.

Interpreting Genesis 2:4–25

Even a brief stroll through Gen. 2:4–25 reveals that this text provides a very different account of creation than the one that immediately precedes it (Gen 1:1–2:3). Where Gen. 1:1–2:3 is focused in its framing of creation in day-length units, Gen. 2:4–25 makes no reference to time in this way. Gen. 2:4–25 tells its story in sequence, but it is unconcerned with marking the passage of time with particular temporal units. God, moreover, is referred to differently in these accounts. Gen 1:1–2:3 uses the term "Elohim" (God) whereas Gen. 2:4–25 uses the compound designation "YHWH Elohim." The God of Gen. 2:4–25 is also far more anthropomorphic (i.e., presented in human form), fashioning the first human out of the soil (v. 7), planting a garden (v. 8), and even performing surgery (vv. 21–22).

The events of creation even occur in a different sequence. In Gen. 1:1–2:3, the creation of animals (vv. 20–25) precedes the creation of the first human couple (vv. 26–27), while in Genesis 2:4–25 the creation of the animals happens in response to the first human's loneliness (2:19–20). And finally, when humans are created in Gen. 2:4–25, they are created at different times (Gen. 2:7, 18–22), whereas Gen. 1:1–2:3 imagines a simultaneous act of creation (Gen. 1:26–27). For the vast majority of scholars, these literary features indicate that Gen. 1:1–2:3 and 2:4–25 were written by different authors/editors at different times for different purposes. The former was written by an exilic, sixth-century source, while the latter's date is highly disputed. It is on Gen. 2:4–25 that we will focus our exegetical energies.

After opening with a generational formula ("These are the generations of the heavens and the earth," see also Gen. 5:1; 6:9; 10:1), the account describes a primordial land, unworked by God or humans (vv. 5–6). These verses leave a subtle hint about the intimate relationship between the flourishing of creation and human care for the earth: the flourishing of the ground was dependent both on God and on the human. Creation is an interconnected, relational web, in which the well-being of one creature is deeply dependent upon the actions of another.

The first human (ha'adam) is formed from the soil (ha'adamah, Gen. 2:7). His derivation from the soil indicates not a relationship of subordination but rather of interconnection, intimacy, and reciprocity. The earth is not only our beginning but also our future home (Gen. 3:19). The vitality of the human depends upon the vitality of the earth and vice versa. With attention to both beauty and sustenance (Gen. 2:9), the Lord God plants a garden and charges this first human creature with its care and protection (Gen. 2:15). God provides the new creation with gifts to sustain life and commands to protect it (Gen. 2:16–17).

But despite this idyllic scene, there are problems in paradise. Beauty, food, and even God were not enough for the first human creature. He was created with a longing for a companion. He was alone, and this was not good (Gen. 2:18). God's first attempt, however, was met with limited success. God brought all of the animals to him, in hopes that they would fulfill the longing for companionship, but to no avail. Back to the drawing board.

In God's second attempt, God creates not from the "ground up," as God did with the animals (Gen. 2:19), but rather using material taken from the side of the first human (Gen. 2:21–22). Just as the first human was derived from the soil, so his companion, the woman, was derived from him, not to communicate her subordination but rather to indicate intimacy and interconnection. Bursting into the Bible's first poem (Gen. 2:23), the man is destabilized: on the one hand, he sees himself in her ("bone of my bone . . . flesh of my flesh," Gen. 2:23), and on the other hand, he finds himself confronted with someone who is genuinely an "other" (she is given a different name, "woman," Gen. 2:23). Recognition and wonder, comfort and disturbance, attraction and alterity—all of these things come together in the first encounter between man and woman. For Genesis 2, this story is an interpretation of marriage (Gen. 2:24), accounting for both its beginnings and its contemporary dynamics.

If we were to continue reading into Genesis 3, we would soon discover that the intricate web of relationships formed in Gen. 2:4–25 quickly comes under threat. Less a fall from grace and more a falling "apart" or falling "out,"[4] the first couples' disobedience sends a shockwave throughout creation (Gen. 3:14–19), resulting in the expulsion of the first couple from the garden. This tragic event foreshadows the conclusion to the broader narrative that Genesis introduces, namely the Enneateuch (Genesis–Kings), which ends with the destruction of Jerusalem and the exile of many Judahites to Babylonia (2 Kings 24–25).

Conclusion

Gen. 2:4–25 is not only a beautiful, well-crafted, and theologically potent story; it is also *true*. This story speaks in penetrating and revelatory ways about the complex relational web among God, creation, and the human. Also underscored is the need to tend to these relationships in meaningful and serious ways, for to neglect them is to invite destruction into God's world.

The God of this creation account is also not the God of traditional Christian theology. The God of Gen. 2:4–25 is a God who responds to new situations, experiments, fails, and learns. Traditional Christian theology imagines a God who is outside of time, all powerful, and aware of all things, past, present, and future. The anthropomorphic representation of God in Gen. 2:4–25, however, while fascinating, is not the only representation of God in Scripture. It is one among many. Keeping this observation in mind, readers should take this opportunity to consider the consequences for Christian theology of a God who exists within time as opposed to outside of it.

Is Gen. 2:4–25 true in the same way that, say, a textbook on cosmology is true? No. Both tell truth, but their respective truths only come to light when one recognizes and respects the questions they are trying to answer. Gen. 2:4–25 is interested in questions like the following: Why do we exist? Why do we long so deeply for human companionship? How are humans called to interact with the earth? Why is our world the way it is (see especially Genesis 3)? Who is God, and what is God like? How does God relate to humanity?

The next chapter looks at yet another way of communicating God's truth: law.

 Notes

1. Cf. Jon Levenson, *Esther* (OTL; Louisville: Westminster John Knox, 1997), 26.

2. Mark A. Throntveit and Alan G. Padgett, "Reading the Bible after Darwin," *Word and World* 29 (2009): 46.

3. Stephen Hawking, *A Brief History of Time: From the Big Bang to Black Holes* (Toronto, New York: Bantam Books, 1988).

4. Terence E. Fretheim, "Is Genesis 3 a Fall Story?," *Word and World* 14 (1994):144–53.

Chapter 9

How Do We Read Biblical Law?

The author of Psalm 119 begins his acrostic poem with lavish praise for God's law:

> Happy are those whose way is blameless,
>> who walk in the law of the Lord.
> Happy are those who keep his decrees,
>> who seek him with their whole heart,
> who also do no wrong,
>> but walk in his ways.
> You have commanded your precepts
>> to be kept diligently.
> O that my ways may be steadfast
>> in keeping your statutes!
> Then I shall not be put to shame,
>> having my eyes fixed on all your commandments.
> I will praise you with an upright heart,
>> when I learn your righteous ordinances.
> I will observe your statutes;
>> do not utterly forsake me. (Ps. 119:1–8)

For ancient Israel, law came from on high. It was "the law of the *Lord*," who is its author. Keeping this law brought happiness and helped one avoid shame. For Israel, the law was a source of deep joy.

The law was given to Israel at Sinai and served to structure the fledgling nation's relationship to their God. Sinai does not mark the beginning of God's relationship to Israel. No, that began in Genesis with the family of Abraham and Sarah (Gen. 12:1–10). The giving of the law did, however, mark a significant shift in Israel's relationship to God. The nation of Israel was to be set apart by God, a "priestly kingdom" and a "holy nation" (Exod. 19:6). The law was also given for Israel's own well-being, so that life would go well for them in the Promised Land (Deut. 4:40; 5:16, 29, 33; 6:3, 18; 10:13; etc.). Law serves life.

Contrary to popular Christian caricatures of Judaism, the law was not given as a way for Israel to be "saved." In many ways, the category of "saved," as it is often used by Christians, did not even exist in ancient Israel. The law set Israel apart as holy among the nations and also provided a way for Israel to "live well," but never was it intended as a path to salvation as Christians often understand the term.

The claim that God authored Israelite law is of deep significance and sets Israel apart among its neighbors. Surrounding nations, of course, had laws of their own. Thanks to archaeology, we know that Israel's legal material often parallels material found elsewhere in the ancient Near East. So similar are some of these laws that many scholars think that Israel actually borrowed and modified laws from their neighbors (cf. especially the Code of Hammurabi and Exod. 20:22–23:33). While Israel's laws may not be unique, its claim that God authored the law certainly is. The more typical pattern was for kings, not gods, to provide laws for their people.

In addition to being theologically significant, the law is also literarily significant. The reception of the law at Sinai is the literary center of the books of Moses. The people of Israel begin to receive the law at Sinai in Exodus 19 and only leave that experience in Numbers 10! Just before Israel crosses into Sinai, and just prior to his death, Moses recites the law again, in a sort of farewell address in Deuteronomy.

The significance of pentateuchal law to Judaism, ancient and modern, cannot be overstated. And it is for this reason that Matthew's Jesus takes upon himself the mantle of Moses and offers a remarkable exposition on the law, known in common parlance as the Sermon on the Mount (Matt. 5–7; cf. Luke 6:20–49). The law also plays a particularly important, albeit complex, role in the writings of Paul (see especially Romans and Galatians).

He would strongly affirm the goodness of the law and its theological significance, not only to Jews but also to Gentiles.

Biblical law comes in various literary forms. Most will be familiar with the "Decalogue" or "Ten Commandments" (Exod. 20:1–21; Deut. 5:6–21), which provides a list of legal commands and unconditional statements related to both the religious and interpersonal dimensions of life. Other collections provide lists of "case" law, which make reference to very specific legal scenarios (e.g., Exod. 20:22–23:33). The book of Deuteronomy is unique in that it is framed as a speech from Moses and is, therefore, hortatory or preached law. Prophets like Jeremiah lament the breaking of God's law (Jer. 5:5; 9:13; 16:11). Legal material even crops up in narrative (see, e.g., 2 Kgs. 22:3–20).

Finally, it is important for Christians to recognize that biblical law is dynamic, not static. The dynamic nature of biblical law is suggested by the fact that the law given at Sinai, Israel's most significant legal corpus, is actually embedded within *narrative*.[1] Law is integrated into a dynamic and sometimes circuitous story line, whose characters are often forced to adapt to new and changing circumstances. Throughout these changing circumstances, God's law proves to be adaptive, not unchanging.

The adaptive nature of law is clearly illustrated in Numbers 27, where the five daughters of Zelophehad plead with Moses to allow them to receive their father's inheritance.[2] The daughters approach Moses and the entire congregation of Israel, saying, "Our father died in the wilderness . . . and he has left no sons. Let not our father's name be lost to his clan just because he had no son! Give us a holding among our father's kinsmen!" (Num. 27:1–4). Full appreciation of their request requires one to recognize what cultural values, assumptions, and traditions give rise to this legal conflict. To die without a son was considered to be a tragedy, in large part because the father's name would be lost to history. So disturbing was this outcome in ancient Israel that a specific law was created to address situations in which a married man died sonless (Deut. 25:5–10). The value of sons in keeping the name of the father in memory and alive is underscored in 2 Samuel 18, in which Absalom erects a monument to his own name in the King's Valley. His reason? "I have no son to keep my name in remembrance" (2 Sam. 18:18). Taking matters into his own hands, Absalom ensures that he will not go to his death forgotten. Numbers 27 relates a story in which the daughters of Zelophehad approach Moses in order to prevent the loss of their father's name. We misread their actions if we see their request as mere selfish squabbling over their father's possessions. In Numbers 27, two competing values stand in conflict: the deeply felt need for the father's name to continue and a particular set of laws and customs in which only men, and sons in particular, could inherit.

Perceiving this conflict, Moses approaches God (Num. 27:5–6), who sides with the daughters. What results from Moses's legal consultation with God, however, is not a "narrow" ruling in favor only of the daughters of Zelophehad but in fact a complete revision of inheritance laws that allows all daughters to inherit from their fathers when there is no son (Num. 27:8–11).

New circumstances that bring deeply held Israelite values into conflict with one another require a new discernment process that involves: (1) hearing the testimony of those adversely affected by the old law, (2) prayer, and (3) ultimately the issuance of a revised law. What this story makes abundantly clear is that biblical law, though authored by God, can also undergo revision.

Reading biblical law can be tedious at times. Israel's scribes had a careful eye for detail and a deep respect for the law they were recording—after all, their task was to pen divine revelation.

The discerning reader, however, will detect in Israel's laws a robust theology of divine revelation and presence, a concern for the nation's well-being in the land, along with the acknowledgment that Israel's law, though divine, was nonetheless responsive to new and changing realities. The law, like God, accompanied Israel on the journey.

©⦾ Notes

1. Terence E. Fretheim, "Law in the Service of Life: A Dynamic Understanding of Law in Deuteronomy," *A God So Near: Essays on Old Testament Theology in Honor of Patrick D. Miller*, ed. Brent A. Strawn and Nancy R. Bowen (Winona Lake, IN: Eisenbrauns, 2003), 183–200.

2. Other examples could be used, especially from Deuteronomy. For an insightful discussion of inner-biblical legal revision, see especially Bernard M. Levinson, *Deuteronomy and the Hermeneutics of Legal Innovation* (Oxford, UK: Oxford University Press, 1997).

Chapter 10

How Do We Read Biblical Poetry?

To be a great reader of the Bible, one must be a great reader of poetry. Most of the Bible's poetry is contained within the Hebrew Bible, where poems comprise about one-third of the texts.[1] The vast majority of poems are found in books like Psalms, Isaiah, Jeremiah, Job, Proverbs, Hosea, Joel, Amos, and Song of Songs. As this list indicates, poetry is found in everything from hymns to prophecy, wisdom books to erotic love literature. Poetry cuts across genres, making it all the more important for readers of the Bible.

Poetry is present in the New Testament, albeit to a lesser degree. One thinks, for instance, of the Christ hymn (Phil. 2:6–11), Mary's *Magnificat* (Luke 1:46–56), Zechariah's prophecy (Luke 1:67–80), numerous citations of Psalms (e.g., Mark 15:34; Matt. 27:46; Heb. 1:5–13), and the hymns of Revelation (e.g., Rev. 4:8, 11; 5:9–13). One can even find quotations of Greek poets in the New Testament. In Acts 17:28, for instance, Paul draws on Greek poets to make an argument to an Athenian audience. Clearly, poetry is not as prominent in the New Testament as it is in the Hebrew Bible. And when the New Testament does contain poetry, it is more often than not a citation from the Hebrew Bible. For these reasons, most of our attention in this chapter will be on the poetry of the Hebrew Bible.

Recognizing Poetry

Because biblical poetry is primarily found in the Hebrew Bible, this chapter will focus on that corpus. There is no single literary feature that defines

Hebrew poetry. Taken as a whole, however, Hebrew poems often exhibit a set of common features that help us identify them as poetry. In this section we explore the most common features.

Let's begin with Ps. 18:1–5:

> I love you, O Lord, my strength.

> The Lord is my rock, my fortress, and my deliverer,
>> my God, my rock in whom I take refuge,
>>> my shield, and the horn of my salvation, my stronghold.

> I call upon the Lord, who is worthy to be praised,
>> so I shall be saved from my enemies.

> The cords of death encompassed me;
>> the torrents of perdition assailed me;

> the cords of Sheol entangled me;
>> the snares of death confronted me.

The first thing to notice is the way that the lines are presented on the page. Each line is surrounded by a significant amount of white space. Translators and publishers use this negative space to indicate that a text is a poem, as opposed to prose, which fills the page from margin to margin (cf. 1 Sam. 2:1–10 [poem] and 1 Sam. 2:11–36 [prose]). This formatting technique communicates visually something the Hebrew poets attempt to communicate literarily: lineation.[2] Lineation is one of the most widespread and significant features of Hebrew poetry.

Parallelism is one of the most common ways that Hebrew poets marked the beginnings and endings of lines (lineation). According to Adele Berlin, parallelism is "the repetition of similar or related semantic content or grammatical structure in adjacent lines or verses."[3] At a fundamental level, parallelism concerns a literary relationship between two lines of poetry. To understand this relationship, one can ask the following questions: When these two lines are compared, what is similar? What is different? Where and how is the first line echoed, modified, advanced, and so on, in the second? Psalm 18:4 again provides an excellent example:

> The cords of death encompassed me;
>> the torrents of perdition assailed me;

Parallelism is at play here in several ways. You might notice, for instance, that the poet ("me") is the object of two verbs ("encompassed me . . . assailed me"). The poet is depicted as a victim of powerful forces—"cords of death" and "torrents of perdition." The first assailant brings to mind the ropes used against a captured animal, which is now at the mercy of hunters. The second assailant is described in watery terms—a common image of chaos in the ancient Near East. Read together, these two parallel lines indicate that the author is not only pursued to the brink of death, but he also stands on the edge of chaos, which threatens to undo him. These lines communicate in vivid terms the poet's deep sense of vulnerability. Identifying these instances of parallelism also helps one identity where lines begin and where they end; that is, they help in spotting lineation.

You may have also noticed that Psalm 18 makes abundant use of imagery. Density of imagery is another strong indicator that one is reading Hebrew poetry. Let's return for the moment to Ps. 18:2:

> The Lord is my rock, my fortress, and my deliverer,
>> my God, my rock in whom I take refuge,
>>> my shield, and the horn of my salvation, my stronghold.

Seven images in a matter of three lines of poetry! God is a rock, a fortress, a deliverer, a rock of refuge, a shield, a horn, a stronghold. Even a brief perusal through the Psalter indicates that it is a veritable encyclopedia of imagery,[4] taken from all aspects of life.

The profound flexibility of divine imagery in this psalm alone raises interesting questions about gender and divine representation. Although the God of the Hebrew Bible is primarily depicted in culturally masculine terms, Hebrew poetry occasionally moves beyond these boundaries to depict God in culturally feminine terms. Deuteronomy 32:18, for instance, claims that God writhed in birth pains to bring forth the chosen nation. Isaiah 42:14, similarly, depicts God as a woman in labor, and Isa. 66:13 also casts God in the guise of a maternal comforter. Psalm 22:9 puts God into the role of a midwife, whereas Ps. 123:2 imagines a God who is like a mistress with handmaidens. These feminine images of God are predominantly found in poetic texts. When reading the poetry of the Hebrew Bible, one often gets the sense that Israel's poets are pushing the boundaries of their language in an effort to communicate the greatness, love, compassion, power, and mercy of their God. The constant stream of new images suggests that Israel never saw its task to bear witness to God as completed, and nei-ther—we might add—should we.

Hebrew poetry also tends to use compressed language. Isaiah 60:1–2 provides an excellent example. These verses read:

> A: Arise, shine; for your light has come,
>   for the glory of the Lord has risen upon you
>
> B: For darkness shall cover the earth,
>   and thick darkness [shall cover] the peoples.

Line A is a rather typical bicolon (two-part line). It contains two verbs ("has come . . . has risen") that are in a parallel relationship to one another. The second verb ("has risen") is far more specific than the first ("has come") and compares God's glory to the rising of the sun. Notice, however, that line B is missing a verb in the second line, indicated by the brackets. This literary device, known as "gapping," omits the verb, all while assuming that the reader can fill the gap on her own.

Proverbial sayings also exhibit similarly compressed language. Proverbs 20:9, for instance, reads:

> Who can say, "I have made my heart clean;
>   I am pure from my sin"?

In the Hebrew text, the question found in the initial line ("Who can say?") is gapped or assumed by the second line, "I am pure from my sin." The assumption by the second line of the question stated in the first raises the artistic register of the proverbs and demonstrates its use of poetic conventions.

You may have already noticed that there are many aspects of Hebrew poetry that are difficult to access apart from some knowledge of biblical languages: Hebrew, Aramaic, and Greek. This is nowhere more apparent than when one studies the role of sound in Hebrew poetry. Israel's poets, like many modern poets, crafted their poetry with careful attention to sound. This was particularly important in Israelite society, which was primarily oral.

The oral artistry of Hebrew poetry, however, is often one of the first casualties of translation. One example comes from Jeremiah's call narrative. God asks the prophet, "What do you see?" (Jer. 1:11). Jeremiah responds, "A branch of an almond tree." God in turn replies, "You have seen well, for I am watching over my word to perform it." Readers unfamiliar with Hebrew will pause and wonder how on earth Jeremiah's reply elicited God's response. The answer is "consonance" or the repetition of consonants. In Hebrew, the word "almond tree" is *shaqed*, and the word "watching over" is *shoqed*. In a vision, Jeremiah is shown an almond tree (*shaqed*), because God is *shoqed*-ing (watching) God's word in order to make sure it comes to pass.

The use of sound in this fashion is found throughout the Hebrew Bible, not only in poetry. Examples like this point to the importance of having some familiarity with original languages. To be sure, one can gain great familiarity with the Bible apart from knowledge of original languages, but one is nonetheless at some disadvantage. Keep in mind that the Bible is the literature of another culture. In the same way that knowledge of Norwegian allows one to appreciate Norway more deeply, knowledge of biblical languages allows one to appreciate the Bible more deeply. Learning languages takes time, energy, and commitment. It is our hope, however, that examples like the one above will motivate you to pursue biblical languages. It is profoundly rewarding to catch poets at work, playing with sounds and semantics, and generally delighting in the potentialities of the Hebrew language.

How to Read a Biblical Poem

To read a poem well is not the same thing as reading, say, an instruction manual well. The skills, goals, and assumptions for reading each are quite different.

Poetry must be read *slowly, patiently, and deliberately.* It's much more like fine dining than it is like fast food. In order to enjoy the fine-dining experience, one needs a mindset that values detail, appreciates the fruits of patience, delights in subtleties, and finds joy in savoring every line. The poets of the Hebrew Scriptures delight in language as language, but catching them in their acts of delight requires careful, patient reading.

One should approach poetry, moreover, not in search of "information," "facts," or "data" but rather in search of an encounter. Modern Christians live in a text-saturated culture, but in most cases, that text is interested in communicating information. Language often is a utilitarian medium. When we approach poetry, however, with utilitarian motives, we meet poetry on terms other than its own and run the risk of missing out on hearing ourselves addressed through the poem. Terry Eagleton, the well-known scholar of English literature, puts it this way: "Poetry is something which is done to us, not just said to us."[5] It turns out that poems are a lot like people: getting to know them requires patience, curiosity, empathy, and concern, not mere utilitarian interest. It is not enough to wonder what a poem is *for*; we must dwell in the artistry and precision of poetic language.

Finally, many Hebrew poems were originally oral compositions. They were written to be performed, not read silently. Some poems were spoken by prophets (see, e.g., Isa. 5:1–7), and some were probably read responsively as part of Israel's cult (e.g., Psalm 118). Another way of gaining appreciation for Hebrew poetry, then, is to read it aloud, either alone or in community. When doing so, attempt through your reading to draw attention to features like parallelism, word play, and lineation.

Poetry and Theology

The Bible presents readers with many challenges, and reading its poetry is among the greatest. Reading biblical poetry is demanding and even frustrating, in large part because to reap the fruits of biblical poetry requires careful, deliberate, and attentive reading habits. Those willing to exercise patience in the reading of poetry, however, will find a plentiful harvest.

But biblical poetry is also significant theologically. In poetry, the God of Israel finds a voice. When Israel's scribes and prophets chose to depict divine speech, they often chose poetry. This is especially true of the prophets, whose words of divine judgment and promise are frequently rendered in poetic lines. For Israel, God is a poet. While those of us who attend Western seminaries will frequently encounter theological texts that are structured like philosophical treatises, we would do well to remember that poetry was one of Israel's chief ways of doing theology. In our view, this fact should push us to consider the theological value, not only of poetry but also of the arts more broadly.

The Gospels also depict Jesus as a reader and speaker of poetry. In Luke 4:14–29, Jesus stands up in his home synagogue, reads an anonymous prophetic poem (Isaiah 61), and boldly declares that said poem was fulfilled in their midst. Like so many of us, Jesus found himself addressed by the ancient words of Scripture. And at the end of his life, Jesus turns again to poetry. While on the cross (Matt. 27:46; Mark 15:34), Jesus quotes a poem, Psalm 22. His words from the cross point us to one of the most influential collections of poetry in Christianity and indeed the Western world: Psalms. At a moment of God-forsakenness, Jesus chose to utter an ancient poem about the lamentable state of the world and of the troubling sense of God's absence. Jesus' own treasuring of poetry encourages us to consider how poetry, and in particular biblical poetry, might help us perceive God's work in the world.

⊙⊙ Notes

1. Chip Dobbs-Allsopp, "Hebrew Poetry," *The New Interpreters Dictionary of the Bible*, 5 vols. (Nashville, TN: Abingdon, 2006–2009), 4:550.

2. For more on lineation, see Shira Wolosky, *The Art of Poetry: How to Read a Poem* (New York: Oxford University Press, 2001), 18.

3. Adele Berlin, "Introduction to Hebrew Poetry," *New Interpreters Bible*, 12 vols. (Nashville, TN: Abingdon, 1994–2004), 4:304.

4. For an excellent study of metaphor in the Psalter, see William P. Brown, *Seeing the Psalms: A Theology of Metaphor* (Louisville, KY: Westminster John Knox, 2001).

5. Terry Eagleton, *How to Read a Poem* (Malden, MA: Blackwell, 2007), 21.

Chapter 11

How Do We Read Prophecy?

Prophets as Messengers

Prophecy is one of the most significant and widespread phenomena in the Bible. Found in both the Hebrew Bible and the New Testament, prophecy is the human attempt to communicate divine messages.[1] Prophets are messengers of God, whose words concern the past, present, and future. The prophets are a diverse bunch. Among their ranks are men and women, Israelite and non-Israelite, true and false, Christian and non-Christian, patronized by the throne and opposed to it. Theologically, economically, and even ethnically diverse, the prophets share one commonality: they see themselves as mouthpieces, called and commissioned to announce God's words.

The notion that prophets are messengers is apparent throughout the Scriptures. To begin with, prophets often preface their prophecies with the phrase, "Thus spoke YHWH" or some variation thereof (see, e.g., Isa. 18:4; 21:6; 30:15; 37:6; 38:1; Jer. 6:16; 17:19; 19:1; 25:15; 35:18; Ezek. 4:13; 11:5; 25:3; Zech. 1:14; 2:8; Obad. 1:1; Mic. 2:3). A similar practice is found in the New Testament (see, e.g., Acts 15:16–17; 21:11).

For the Hebrew Bible, the image of the prophet as messenger is made on analogy with royal messengers, who spoke on behalf of their royal masters. For example, in Isaiah 36 an Assyrian military official, the Rabshakeh, makes this proclamation to King Hezekiah's officials: "The Rabshakeh said to them, 'Say to Hezekiah: *Thus says the great king, the king of Assyria*: On what do you base this confidence of yours?'" (Isa. 36:4 NRSV). It was the role of the messenger to convey the words and will of their master to the intended audience. The prophets, similarly, understood themselves to be royal messengers, commissioned by their king to make pronouncements. As representatives of the divine king, the prophets of the Hebrew Bible were also often involved in the affairs of earthly kings (see 1 Samuel 8–10; 2 Samuel 7, 12, 16; 1 Kings 22; 2 Kings 18–19).

Prophetic messengers continue to play a role in the New Testament as well, not so much in the context of royal politics, as seen above, but rather in the context of church life. Paul, for instance, assumes that prophecy was one among many spiritual gifts, useful primarily for the edification of the church (1 Cor. 14:1–3). And it was assumed by some that ongoing prophetic activity was in fact a sign of God's kingdom (Acts 2:14–21).

Prophets and Tradition

In the popular imagination, prophets are often understood to be isolated social reformers who rejected tradition, "dead" religion, and the past for a new and progressive future of social justice. These caricatures, however, are far removed from the evidence. The prophets, far from rejecting the past, made abundant use of the religious and historical traditions they inherited.

Mark Twain's famous words about plagiarism are just as applicable to the prophets as they are about any other piece of human utterance:

> The kernel, the soul—let us go further and say the substance, the bulk, the actual and valuable material of all human utterances—is plagiarism. For substantially all ideas are second-hand, consciously and unconsciously drawn from a million outside sources, and daily use by the garnerer with a pride and satisfaction born of the superstition that he originated them. . . . When a great orator makes a great speech you are listening to ten centuries and ten thousand men—but we call it his speech, and really some exceedingly small portion of it is his. . . . It takes a thousand men to invent a telegraph, or a steam engine, or a phonograph, or a telephone or any other important thing— and the last man gets the credit and we forget the others.[2]

The prophets are profound, not for their originality, but for the remarkable way in which they reconfigure and recast inherited traditions, and in ways that address the concerns of their own time. In order to understand the profundity of the prophets, then, one needs to look not only to the present they inhabited or the futures they imagined but also to the past traditions that inspired them. The prophets were masters of the remix.

The book of Jeremiah provides some of the most fascinating remixes. Chapter 7 describes a famous sermon given by Jeremiah at the gate of the temple:

> Thus says the Lord of hosts, the God of Israel: Amend your ways and your doings, and let me dwell with you in this place. Do not trust in these deceptive words: "This is the temple of the Lord, the temple of the Lord, the temple of the Lord." For if you truly amend your ways and your doings, if you truly act justly one with another, if you do not oppress the alien, the orphan, and the widow, or shed innocent blood in this place, and if you do not go after other gods to your own hurt, then I will dwell with you in this place, in the land that I gave of old to your ancestors forever and ever. Here you are, trusting in deceptive words to no avail. Will you steal, murder, commit adultery, swear falsely, make offerings to Baal, and go after other gods that you have not known, and then come and stand before me in this house, which is called by my name, and say, "We are safe!"—only to go on doing all these abominations?

The text makes abundant use of inherited traditions. To begin with, Jeremiah accuses his audience of trusting in "deceptive words." His audience is convinced that God will protect not only God's house but also God's people. Their beliefs are not without a foundation. Many psalms and even stories suggest that God is committed to protecting the temple and God's people (e.g., Psalms 46, 48, 76; Isaiah 36–37; 2 Kings 18–19). This theological tradition is associated with the royal ideology of Judah, whose capital was Jerusalem, and is summarized in Ps. 46:5: "God is in the midst of the city; it shall not be moved; God will help it when the morning dawns." Jeremiah does something remarkable, however. Drawing on the theology of Deuteronomy, he transforms these traditions about Zion's invincibility by making their claims dependent upon the people's obedience to God. He doesn't deny that God will protect God's place and people, but he does insist that said protection will only be guaranteed if God's people repent: "For *if* you truly amend your ways and your doings, *if* you truly act justly one with another, *if* you do not oppress the alien, the orphan, and the widow, or shed innocent blood in this place, and *if* you do not go after other gods to your own hurt, *then* I will dwell with you in this place, in the land that I gave of old to your ancestors forever and ever." The promise of protection is conditional.

In order to appreciate more fully the artistry of Jeremiah 7, one must recognize that it is not just a text; it is a remix. Jeremiah's sermon reconfigures traditional material in such a way as to chastise his audience for trusting in deceptive words.

Jeremiah 7 is not the exception but the rule. The brilliance of the biblical prophets lies not in their ability to dream up new ideas but rather in their ability to reconfigure ancient traditions to speak in powerful ways about contemporary realities.

True and False Prophecy

Israel recognized that there were both true and false prophets. Prophecy required evaluation. The discernment of true and false prophecy was relevant both to ancient Israel (see, e.g., Deut. 13:1–5; 18:15–22; 1 Kings 22) and to the New Testament (Acts 13:6; 2 Cor. 11:13; 2 Peter 2:1–3). And it remains relevant to modern Christians, not only because the church's ranks contain Christians who practice prophetic gifts, but also because discerning the voice of truth in all matters of life and faith is a fundamental Christian mandate (Matt. 7:15; 24:4; Mark 13:5; Luke 21:8; 2 Peter 3:17).

Imagine this scene. You are living in early-sixth-century BCE Jerusalem. All the political buzz is about the newest imperial threat on the horizon: Babylon. What will happen to Jerusalem? Should we surrender? Submit? Ally with another neighboring power? What does the king think? With these questions in the air, you walk by the Jerusalem temple and overhear a dispute between two famous prophets. One of them claims that God will unconditionally protect God's temple from foreign invaders. "Don't submit to your Babylonian invaders," they claim, "for this is God's city and God's temple, and it is unshakeable. To quote one of our great poets, 'God is in the midst of the city; it shall not be moved; God will help it when the morning dawns' [Ps. 46:5]." Another less-popular prophet stands to his feet and mocks his prophetic colleague, saying, "Don't trust the words of this deceiver. He is speaking pure lies. This is God's word: Submit to Babylon, for I, YHWH, have handed this precious city of mine over to your enemy, as judgment for your sins. Peace is found in surrender." How would you decide? Which of these prophets is speaking truth? Which one is speaking falsely? The situation described above actually happened in Judah in the early sixth century BCE and is most clearly reflected in the book of Jeremiah (Jeremiah 7; 27).

The Bible provides no easy answers to these questions. Discernment is, to say the least, a messy process. Looking at the Bible holistically, however, one finds a number of criteria, across multiple books, that are significant for evaluating prophecy and, we would add, all attempts to speak on behalf of God. Our summary of these criteria can be found below, along with supporting biblical texts.[3]

1. Is the prophecy in the service of Yahweh or another god?

Jer. 2:8, 26–27; 23:13–15; 32:32–35; Ezek. 13:17–23; 1 Kgs. 18:20–40

For the Bible, prophecy is true only if it is in service of the one true God of Israel, creator of the world. According to Deuteronomy, if a prophet tries to lead the people astray, saying, "Let us follow other gods" (Deut. 13:2), his words should be ignored, even if he accurately predicted omens and portents. For the New Testament, it is supremely important that all truth claims are grounded in "the truth of Christ" (1 Cor. 11:10; 2 Peter 2:1–3), and that prophecy and all other spiritual gifts are exercised in love (1 Cor. 13:2). Prophecy must be marked by faithfulness to God, who is the source of all true prophetic words.

2. Does the prophecy proceed to fulfillment?

Deut. 18:15–22; 28:8–9; Ezek. 33:33

Even though fulfillment is insufficient as a criterion for determining the truthfulness of a prophet or prophecy, it is nonetheless an important criterion, at least for a number of biblical texts, especially when the prophecy concerns a future event.

3. Is the prophecy in accordance with received tradition?

Deut. 13:1–6; Jer. 6:13–17

Modern people are wont to place more trust in that which is new and innovative. The ancient world, however, tended to place a greater degree of trust in ancient sources. It is for this reason that Jeremiah urges his audience to,

> Stand at the crossroads, and look,
>> and ask for the ancient paths,
> where the good way lies; and walk in it,
>> and find rest for your souls.

When evaluating truth claims, then, traditional sources (e.g., creeds, ancient texts) may serve as helpful conversation partners.

4. Is the prophecy appropriate to the situation?

Jer. 7:1–15; 14:13–16; 23:16–17; 28:2–11; Lam. 2:14; Ezek. 13:8–16

This is perhaps one of the most difficult criteria to evaluate. Whether a particular prophetic word is "appropriate" to a situation often cannot be determined until after the fact. And yet, the biblical texts insist that the timing of a prophetic word is just as important as its contents.

In Ezek. 13:9–10, YHWH says, "My hand will be against the prophets who see false visions and utter lying divinations . . . because they have misled my people, saying, 'Peace,' when there is no peace; and because, when the people build a wall, these prophets smear whitewash on it." These false prophets are wrong, not because of the content of their oracles, but because of the timing of their prophecies. They proclaimed an era of peace, when they were living in an age of wrath.

5. Does the prophet's life have integrity?

Jer. 6:13–15; 23:14–15; Ezek. 13:1–5; 22:28–31; Mic. 3:1–5; Matt. 7:15–16

The truthfulness of prophets is not just a matter of their words; it is also about the quality of their lives. In the words of Jeremiah, false prophets are not only false because they speak erroneous words ("They have treated the wound of my people carelessly, saying, 'Peace, peace,' when there is no peace," Jer. 6:14), but also because they are "greedy for unjust gain" (Jer. 6:13). The integrity of the prophet's words is integrally linked to the integrity of the prophet's life.

Matthew's Jesus makes a similar point when, near the end of the Sermon on the Mount, he urges his audience to examine the words of prophets alongside their lives (Matt. 7:15–20). And the way to know whether a prophet is a "sheep" or a "wolf" is to examine the prophet's "fruits" (Matt. 7:16). Fruit, of course, takes time to grow—a fact that may point to the need for patience when attempting to discern the veracity of a prophet's words.

Prophecy and Jesus

Finally, at the center of Christian faith is the assertion that Jesus Christ is the fulfillment of Israelite prophecy. The Nicene Creed is illustrative:

> We believe in the Holy Spirit, the Lord, the giver of life,
> who proceeds from the Father and the Son,
> who with the Father and the Son is worshiped and glorified,
> *who has spoken through the prophets.*

According to the Creed, to hear the voice of the prophets is to hear the voice of the Spirit, the third person of the Trinity, who is worshiped alongside the Father and the Son. The Creed further claims, "On the third day he [Jesus Christ] rose again *in accordance with the scriptures.*" For the Creed and for Christian theology more broadly, Jesus' life, death, and resurrection are not merely significant historical events; they represent the fulfillment of ancient prophetic words.

The Apostles' Creed is not novel in how it thinks about Jesus. Many New Testament texts explicitly claim that Jesus fulfilled divine promises. The Gospel of Matthew is a notable example, with its underscoring of fulfillment quotations (Matt. 1:22; 2:5, 15, 17, 23; 4:14; 8:17; 12:17; 13:35; 21:4; 27:9). After healing a man at the temple, Peter gives a sermon to the gathering crowd, in which he claims that Jesus' death was foretold in "all the prophets" (Acts 3:17; cf. Luke 24:25–27). Many other texts could be cited.

But the Christian belief that Jesus fulfills ancient messianic prophecy raises an important set of questions for modern Christian interpreters. What is the relationship between the New Testament's Christological interpretations of the Hebrew Bible and the interpretations offered by modern historians, who prefer to interpret the prophecy of the Hebrew Bible against its own historical context? Must Christians choose between the historical reconstructions of biblical scholars and the Christian assertion that Israel's promises culminate in Christ?

For early Christians, Jesus' life, death, and resurrection represented a significant turning point in God's relationship with Israel and with the world. In stark contrast to the modern-day division between the God of the Hebrew Bible and the God of the New Testament, the authors of the New Testament saw deep and profound continuity between the God of Israel and the God of Jesus of Nazareth—in fact, the two were one and the same. The story of Israel, beginning with the ancestors in Genesis, continued on in the person of Christ. In all aspects of his life, Jesus represented prophetic hope and fulfillment.

These claims about Christ are crucial to Christian faith, and there is no reason for Christians to set them aside. But readers run into trouble if their interpretations of the Hebrew Bible dismiss or diminish the significance of God's words to Israel in the past. These ancient words, given to and comprehended by Israelites, were no less significant or powerful, no less the word of God, when they were first spoken and believed. To borrow the language of Hebrews:

> In the past God spoke to our ancestors through the prophets at many times and in various ways, but in these last days he has spoken to us by his Son, whom he appointed heir of all things, and through whom also he made the universe. (Heb. 1:1–2)

The same God who spoke to our ancestors in "many and various ways" is the same God who speaks to us now through Christ, his Son. Because of this theological reality, Christians stand to benefit from reading the Hebrew Bible not only against the horizon of Christ but also against the horizon of Israel's own history.

 Notes

1. Martti Nissinen with contributions from C. L. Seow and Robert K. Ritner, *Prophets and Prophecy in the Ancient Near East*, Society of Biblical Literature Writings from the Ancient World (Atlanta, GA: Society of Biblical Literature, 2003), 1.

2. Albert Bigelow Paine, ed., *Mark Twain's Letters*, 2 vols. (New York: Harper & Brothers Publishers, 1917), 2:731.

3. This list is developed from the work of Terence Fretheim. See his *Jeremiah* (Macon, GA: Smyth & Helwys, 2002), 396–98.

Chapter 12

How Do We Read Wisdom Literature?

What kind of world has God created, and how can we thrive in it? What is human well-being? How do we reach it? How can we make sense of life's adversities and anomalies? Who are the wise, and who are the foolish? And how finally do we transmit wisdom to younger generations?[1] Although these may sounds like modern questions, they are in fact the animating concerns of biblical wisdom literature.

When biblical scholars talk about wisdom literature, they are typically referring to Proverbs, Job, Ecclesiastes (aka Qoheleth), along with a number of psalms that feature wisdom themes (e.g., Psalms 37, 49, 73). While the book of James does share some features of these texts (e.g., Jas. 3:13–17), wisdom literature is more common in the Hebrew Bible than in the New Testament.

Up to this point, we've referred to wisdom literature as if it were a singular category. While it is true that wisdom texts orbit around a common set of questions, it would be incorrect to conclude that all wisdom literature responds to these questions in the same way. Like so much of the Bible, wisdom literature is theologically plural. To illustrate the plurality of wisdom literature, let's look at three texts, one from each of the three wisdom books: Proverbs, Job, and Ecclesiastes.

Proverbs 7–8

Every text creates a symbolic world into which the reader is invited, and Proverbs 7–8 is no different. The world it creates is dominated by the voice of a father, who speaks to his silent son with whom the reader is invited to identify. In the process of offering instruction, the father uses women as examples of wisdom and exemplars of foolishness. He represents not only the speech of women but also their lives, bodies, and actions. In service of defining and teaching wisdom, the father uses two female figures—Lady Wisdom and Dame Folly—to "define and secure the boundaries of the symbolic order of patriarchal wisdom."[2] That is, these female characters are seen strictly from the perspective of patriarchal power. It is a man's perspective, and only a man's perspective, that matters in Proverbs. Read in this manner, these chapters serve as a cogent reminder that *all* speech is always caught up in complex networks of power and privilege. We can never escape these networks, but we can be aware of them. And we can notice the way power and privilege works in a book like Proverbs, we can critique these perspective, and yet we can still learn something from these ancient and sometimes troubling texts. In other words, we can acknowledge the complexity of a biblical text, even question its vision while we still keep an open heart that these texts might yet lead us to insights that help us see something new. These texts might reveal the depth of the oppression we experience but also embedded perspectives of our own that might contribute to the oppression of others.

As we know, the Bible is embedded in culture, time, and space. And because of this, the Bible is subject to historical analysis and critical scrutiny. As readers, we are free to read these texts as products of ancient Near Eastern cultures. To read them in this way is to read them honestly and to take seriously the long and complicated process through which these texts emerged—a process, Christians affirm, that was inspired by God. And yet, as Christians, we can also affirm that these texts, like us, are among the many ways in which God uses finite, limited, and even sinful means to accomplish God's work in the world.

With that said, let's turn to Proverbs. With the voice of paternal authority, Proverbs 7–8 describes two women, Dame Folly and Lady Wisdom.[3] The reader is urged to make Lady Wisdom an intimate companion. Her fruit is better than gold, and her paths are righteousness and justice (Prov. 8:19–20). But at all costs, the reader is told to avoid Dame Folly, the "strange woman" whose "smooth words" (Prov. 7:4–5) lead not only to the foolish life but also, more seriously, to death (Prov. 7:23). Proverbs concerns itself with life-and-death choices.

The paternal figure's teaching about the strange woman emerges out of his observation of the world. He has seen many a simple youth drawn to Dame Folly's house of love "at the time of night and darkness" (Prov. 7:9). With seductive words, she urges them to follow her into bed, where they will take their fill of love until morning (Prov. 7:13–20). The highly erotic nature of this description attempts to demonstrate the power of folly's temptation, likening it to a young person's urge for sexual encounters. While her words may sound sweet, the teacher says, the fool who follows her is "like a bird rushing into a snare, not knowing that it will cost him his life" (Prov. 7:23). Her house, in fact, "is the way to Sheol, going down to the chambers of death" (Prov. 7:27).

Lady Wisdom, on the contrary, takes her stand on the heights, beside the way, and at the crossroads. Like Dame Folly, Lady Wisdom also calls out to potential pupils. But in contrast to Dame Folly, Lady Wisdom's words are noble, true, and prudent. Her teaching is the true strength of kings, rulers, and nobles (Prov. 8:15–16). And even though she is the bearer of "riches . . . honor . . . enduring wealth and prosperity" (Prov. 8:18), the reward of her teaching far exceeds wealth (Prov. 8:19). To choose wisdom is to choose life and life abundant. The wise person will have a long existence, an abundance of friends, good health, a house filled with children, and sufficient possessions to carry one through all of life's storms.[4] These blessings are, for Proverbs, the good life.

Taken as a whole, the book of Proverbs imagines two kinds of people: the wise and the foolish. Or, to use the language of Proverbs 7–8, one can either follow Lady Wisdom to righteousness, truth, and knowledge, or one can follow Dame Folly to the "chambers of death" (Prov. 7:27). What happens, however, when one faithfully follows Lady Wisdom but still ends up with a life full of dreadful consequences? This is precisely the question driving the book of Job.

The Book of Job

Job is the paragon of wisdom. Job was "blameless and upright, and one who feared God and turned away from evil" (Job 1:1). He also experienced the benefits of a wise life, including abundant children and resources. Due to a heavenly conspiracy, however, Job is afflicted by "the satan." This character is not the devil of the New Testament or of modern popular imagination but rather a regular member of God's court who was charged with offering contrarian opinions. That is, the satan is a literary figure in a mythical court.

Job is given into the hands of the satan, and nearly all of the external markers of a wise life (e.g., wealth, children, health) are taken away. The traditional relationship between wisdom and blessing is hereby called into question. Job is wise and is the "greatest of all the people of the east" (Job 1:3), and yet he suffers unimaginable losses. But why?

Job insists throughout that he is innocent and undeserving of the suffering he is experiencing. But his friends, assuming that Job's dreadful circumstances result from his sin, offer an array of contrary diagnoses. The first speech is from Eliphaz, one of Job's friends:

> Think now, who that was innocent ever perished?
>> Or where were the upright cut off?
> As I have seen, those who plow iniquity
>> and sow trouble reap the same.
> By the breath of God they perish,
>> and by the blast of his anger they are consumed. (Job 4:7–9)

Job replies by inviting his friends to find any sin in him:
> But now, be pleased to look at me;
>> for I will not lie to your face.
> Turn, I pray, let no wrong be done.
>> Turn now, my vindication is at stake.
> Is there any wrong on my tongue?
>> Cannot my taste discern calamity? (Job 6:28–30)

Job and his friends go back and forth, with Job insisting on his innocence and his friends, in a variety of ways, insisting that he is in the wrong—until finally, God appears "out of the whirlwind" (Job 38:1). Job will, after all, get his day in court.

God takes Job on a whirlwind tour of creation, asking the broken Job a flurry of questions, all of which are centered on God's work in creation:

> Where were you when I laid the foundation of the earth?
>> Tell me, if you have understanding.
> Who determined its measurements—surely you know!
>> Or who stretched the line upon it?

On what were its bases sunk,
> or who laid its cornerstone
when the morning stars sang together
> and all the heavenly beings shouted for joy? (Job 38:4–7)

God's lengthy speech to Job extends from 38:1 to 41:34. These speeches are literarily and theologically rich. One thing that comes through clearly, however, is that humanity is not at the center of creation.[5] In fact, creatures exist that are more powerful than humans and that even mock or threaten human existence. One thinks for instance of the ostrich, which "When spreads its plumes aloft, it laughs at the horse and its rider" (Job 39:18). And then there are Behemoth and Leviathan. Of Behemoth it is said,

It is the first of the great acts of God—
> only its Maker can approach it with the sword . . .
Even if the river is turbulent, it is not frightened;
> it is confident though Jordan rushes against its mouth.
Can one take it with hooks
> or pierce its nose with a snare? (Job 40:19, 23–24)

The chaos monster, Leviathan, is hymned by none other than God. The hymn begins with a series of questions indicating humanity's utter weakness before the powerful creature:

Can you draw out Leviathan with a fishhook,
> or press down its tongue with a cord?
Can you put a rope in its nose,
> or pierce its jaw with a hook?
Will it make many supplications to you?
> Will it speak soft words to you?
Will it make a covenant with you
> to be taken as your servant forever?
Will you play with it as with a bird,
> or will you put it on leash for your girls?
Will traders bargain over it?
> Will they divide it up among the merchants?
Can you fill its skin with harpoons,
> or its head with fishing spears?
Lay hands on it;

> think of the battle; you will not do it again!
> Any hope of capturing it will be disappointed;
>> were not even the gods overwhelmed at the sight of it?
> No one is so fierce as to dare to stir it up.
>> Who can stand before it?
> Who can confront it and be safe?
>> —under the whole heaven, who?

What kind of answer is this to Job's many supplications, accusations, and questions? It is an answer that demonstrates that Job exists in a cosmos of creatures. Some of these creatures can be domesticated (Job 1:3), but some cannot and will continue to pose a threat to humanity (e.g., Leviathan and Behemoth). There are forces of chaos in this world that, despite human morality, despite human civilization, will nonetheless break out in profoundly destructive ways. Job finally accepts that reality and his place in it. And now knowing the risks of a world inhabited by Behemoth and Leviathan, he nonetheless chooses to exercise profound courage by having children again (Job 42:13–14).

Ecclesiastes 2

The last set of texts we want to explore are from Ecclesiastes 2. Here, the teacher relates a numbers of life experiments he did to determine how "to appraise wisdom and to appraise madness and folly" (Eccl. 1:17). Ultimately, he is interested in knowing "what was good for mortals to do under heaven during the few days of their life" (Eccl. 2:3). He begins by saying to himself, "Come now, I will make a test of pleasure; enjoy yourself" (Eccl. 2:1). He pursues this experiment by seeking pleasure in a whole range of activities and acquisitions:

- Wine (v. 3)
- Building houses, planting vineyards, and creating idyllic settings (vv. 4–5)
- A labor force that works for him (v. 7, 8)
- Livestock (v. 7)
- Silver and gold (v. 8)
- Delights of the flesh (v. 8)
- Concubines (v. 8)

- Greatness (v. 9)
- Wisdom (v. 9)
- Whatever his eyes desired (v. 10)
- Toil (v. 10)

Looking back on his lavish royal life and reflecting on "all that my hands had done and the toil I had spent in doing it," he concludes that "all was vanity and chasing after the wind, and there was nothing gained under the sun" (Eccl. 2:11).

Finding nothing but folly, he turns now to the topics of "wisdom and madness and folly" (Eccl. 2:12). He concludes that "wisdom excels folly as light excels darkness" (Eccl. 2:13). And yet, "the same fate befalls all of them" (that is, wise and foolish alike, Eccl. 2:14). Both the wise and the foolish die. Neither escapes death, and both will eventually be forgotten (Eccl. 2:15–16). One's toil, moreover, is also vanity and chasing after the wind, because it will be enjoyed by others, who may be wise or foolish. In despair, he cries, "What do mortals get from all the toil and strain with which they toil under the sun? For all their days are full of pain, and their work is a vexation; even at night their minds do not rest" (Eccl. 2:22–23).

Closed in and frustrated on every side by futility and mortality, Qoheleth finally stumbles upon an insight, one that embraces the pleasures of life but recognize these as gift of God. "There is nothing better for mortals than to eat and drink, and find enjoyment in their toil. This also, I saw, is from the hand of God; for apart from him who can eat or who can have enjoyment?" (Eccl. 2:24). Qoheleth's conclusions about the fleeting nature of pleasure are correct, so one should enjoy the pleasurable gifts of God while one has them.

Reflecting Theologically on Wisdom Literature

At the heart of wisdom literature is exploration of the world, not for its own sake, but for the sake of learning how to live prudently and successfully in God's world. And although thoroughly ancient in their methods, certain wisdom texts approach the world in ways that will resonate among modern people. For example, Ecclesiastes employs experimentation, and Proverbs leans heavily on observational insight, even observation of the animals (Prov. 30:24–31). Wisdom literature does not typically come from visions, heavenly voices, or angels but rather from human reflection on the world.[6] While none of these texts are properly scientific or modern, they nonetheless share with modernity an appreciation for the human capacity to distill wisdom from observation or experimentation on the perceptible world.

The underlying theological assumption of most wisdom literature is that God has created a world whose patterns and structures are comprehensible and accessible to human inquiry. Lady Wisdom, to use the language of Proverbs, was there from the beginning (Prov. 8:22–36), and her ways are apparent even today, especially to those who fear the Lord (Prov. 1:7). To embrace wisdom is to embrace life, and to ignore wisdom is to choose death (Prov. 8:36). And the only prerequisite to such wisdom is that one must be willing to listen.

And yet, the world is not simply there to be comprehended, discovered, and in turn exploited. Sometimes the world pushes back. Israel's sages make space for forces that cannot be contained or subdued by human hands (e.g., Behemoth and Leviathan in Job 40–41). The world is overflowing with insight, but it is also dangerous; the world is not made for humans alone.

Wisdom literature is stunningly universal in its scope. And this is not only because it is grounded in creation but also because it generally lacks reference to Israel's own national story or experience. Keep in mind that one of the greatest figures of wisdom, Job, is not an Israelite, but rather a man from "Uz" (Job 1:1). Job is every person, and the lessons he learns belong to all of us.

◯⊙◯ Notes

1. See James L. Crenshaw, *Old Testament Wisdom: An Introduction*, 3rd ed. (Louisville: Westminster John Knox Press, 2010), 4.

2. Ibid.

3. Many of the insights shared here are inspired by Carol A. Newsom, "Woman and the Discourse of Patriarchal Wisdom: A Study of Proverbs 1–9," in *Gender and Difference in Ancient Israel*, ed. Peggy Day (Minneapolis: Fortress Press, 1989), 142–60.

4. See Crenshaw, *Old Testament Wisdom*, 72.

5. The work of Kathryn Schifferdecker is of particular significance here. See her *Out of the Whirlwind: Creation Theology in the Book of Job*, Harvard Theological Studies (Cambridge MA: Harvard University Press, 2008).

6. The divine speeches at the end of Job are an important exception to this statement (Job 38–41).

Chapter 13

How Do We Read Narratives?

A ccording to Luke 15, the Pharisees and the scribes disapproved of the company Jesus kept when he ate. These Pharisees and scribes "grumbled" that Jesus was breaking bread and sharing wine with "tax collectors and sinners." In short, Jesus was eating with the wrong kind of people. In fact, I'm often tempted to replace the term "sinners" in the Gospels with the phrase "*those* people," as in those people with which most of us would not want to associate.[1]

Luke's Jesus clearly sees things differently and seeks to help elucidate a different way that we might see those others, *those people* we would prefer to ignore in our everyday lives. He very well could have started preaching here like he does in the Sermon on the Mount in Matthew or the Sermon on the Plain in Luke, detailing how the poor and the broken and the weak and the sinful are beloved by the God who blesses them. He could have detailed a list of behaviors that faithful followers of God ought to embrace, perhaps something akin to the practical wisdom of the book of James. He could have listed some rules to follow in our interactions with those sinners and tax collectors we encounter in our own lives.

Instead, he shatters our expectations by telling three stories, three stories so powerful that many people know them even if they have never opened a Bible in their lives.

First, he tells a story about a shepherd with a hundred sheep. He loses one. He searches frantically for it. He finds it. He throws a big party to celebrate. And then Jesus explains how heaven itself throws a party when any sinner repents but not so much over ninety-nine people who are already righteous.

And then he tells another story. There was a woman with ten coins. She loses one. She searches frantically for it. She finds it. She throws a big party to celebrate. And then Jesus explains how heaven itself throws a party when any sinner repents.

Did you notice the pattern?

Both stories are built in parallel with similar components leading to the same conclusion. Both narrate someone who has lost something precious and how his or her finding what was once lost precipitates a ridiculous, outsized celebration. And both address the concern of the Pharisees and scribes. You've got things backward, Jesus tells them with these stories. These sinners are welcomed by God and thus by me too. But he tells them this with a story, not a declaration, with narratives that linger in the memory rather than instructions we might choose to neglect.

But that's not the end; Jesus tells a third story. We should again expect the same pattern. And to a large extent, the story of the prodigal son, as it is commonly known, follows the pattern of the story of the shepherd who loses a sheep and a woman who loses a coin. But we notice quickly that the pattern breaks in at least one respect. This is a much longer, more complex story. Already, we, as readers or listeners, should know something is about to change.

So, Jesus tells a story about a man who loses a son. This younger son asks for his inheritance and quickly heads off to a foreign land, where he spends all his recently acquired cash and is caught up in the wake of a famine. No one helps him. Hungry, destitute, and desperate, he figures he might as well head home. After all, his father's house—even despite the consternation he must have caused his father—is better than this! And so he heads back, rehearsing an apology he will share with his father. But his father has never stopped looking over the horizon for him.

In his own way, this father has looked for his lost son as the shepherd looked for the sheep and the woman the coin. In fact, this young man may have been more like the sheep and coin than he could have known. He probably didn't know how lost he truly was.

So, a father loses a son. He searches for him frantically. He finds him again, even interrupting his son's rehearsed apology! And then the father throws a big, outsized, ridiculous party. And that should be the end of the story. This is exactly how the other two stories ended.

But we might have forgotten about the older brother working in the fields. His reintroduction to this story is like a needle scratching across the surface of a record. His arrival at this party throws the story on its head. When he returns, he is furious that his father has thrown a party for such an ingrate. These brothers are not exactly on speaking terms at the moment! The older brother won't even refer to "my brother" but only "your son." The father comes outside pleading with his older son. Your brother, he says, was as good as dead. Now he has come back to life. We had to throw this party.

Three memorable stories, but why does Jesus choose to respond in this way? Why tell two simple stories with a powerful message only to introduce a third, more complicated story? What is he trying to do and say?

After all, it would have been simpler for Jesus to explain to these Pharisees and scribes that they ought not view their neighbors through the prism of their occupations or whether they made for worthy company. He could have pointed to these sinners and tax collectors and observed that they too are children of Abraham like he proclaims when crowds later in Luke similarly object to the company Jesus keeps (see Luke 19:10).

Why tell a story? We might ask the question about the Gospels as a whole. Why did the authors of Matthew, Mark, Luke, and John choose to tell stories about Jesus' life? We might ask the same of the composers, editors, and collectors of the Pentateuch, the first five books of the Hebrew Scriptures.

In one way, we can answer these questions pretty easily. Of course, our Bibles are full of stories. They were written by humans, after all. Humans are storytellers. This is what we do! Whether we are writing books or sitting around a campfire, we frame our lives around stories more than mere facts, narratives more than data about our lives. This is another way that Scripture comes alive as a text composed with human hands and breathed by God's Spirit.

Why do we tell stories? Partly we engage in the weaving of narratives because they are delightful, entertaining, and poignant. Stories, when told well, are lively and exciting. I ask my children to tell me their stories about their days in school because that tells me so much more than words like *fine* or *good* that follow the question, "How was your day?" In this way, stories can tell us so much more. They can enliven and color the ordinariness of life with possibility and wonder.

But storytelling, notice, is about us, the people who share in this fundamentally human act. First, the storyteller is as important as the story itself. That is, how the storyteller shapes the story matters. What is her tone of voice? What is her pace? Does she tell the story in chronological order or as a series of flashbacks? Does she tell the story in past tense or present tense? Second, the audience too is as important as the story itself. Does the audience or the storyteller trust what they are hearing? Does the audience want to hear this story, or do they feel duty bound to do so? Are they listening intently or merely enduring the story? What will the audience do with the story they receive?

We are wired to tell and listen to stories, much like we are wired to delight in the patterns of poetry and the rhythms of music. To me, therefore, it is a source of delight that we hear about Jesus in these lively Gospel narratives, that we learn about the dawn of God's creativity in vibrant story form in Genesis, that we lament the depths of our brokenness in the "texts of terror" found in Judges.[2]

So how do we approach narrative differently than we might approach a text that includes legal codes or poetry or apocalyptic visions? Let's start with four basic guidelines for this kind of reading.

1. Respect the Integrity of the World the Narrative Creates

Part of the power of storytelling is that stories ask us to immerse ourselves in a new world. We can see this clearly with fantasy literature. J. K. Rowling invites us to consider a world where wizards and witches go to a boarding school dedicated to the craft of magic. J. R. R. Tolkien concocts worlds populated with hobbits and orcs and elves and a ring of power. The story would not work if we didn't believe, even if but for a moment, the worlds they narrate. If in some way, we refused to dispense the knowledge that the adventures of Harry Potter and Frodo Baggins alike are conceits, fictions we buy into for the sake of seeing the world these two fabulous imaginations have shared with us, then these stories would lose all their power. If we allow the thought that these stories are implausible or unreal, then the imagination required of us collapses. This suspension of disbelief is an agreement between author and reader. I will trust you, the reader says to the storyteller, to take me to this world. I will buy into this world and see where it takes me.

Every narrative, every story projects a world. Every narrative, every story creates scenarios and environments and situations. Even my children's stories about their day at school requires me to see the world as they see it for the moment, to see childhood dilemmas as significant and not merely as so much childlike drama.

So, when we turn to the narratives of Scripture, we should respect the integrity of the world the narrative creates. This does not eliminate the possibility of critique and questioning; that is, we do not need simply to accept the world these narratives create. It does mean, however, that we allow the author to take us to a literary world we may find strange and unfamiliar and perhaps even dangerous. The ancient world was quite different than our own, to say the least. Assumptions about the basics of life would seem strange to us. In fact, some of those assumptions may be at odds with our own assumptions. Despite all this, we ought to remember that there is an integrity to these narrative worlds even if that integrity strikes us as odd, even deeply problematic.

In short, enter the world the narrative creates. Spend some time wandering in the worlds Mark and Matthew and the other authors and editors of the Bible concocted.

2. Discern the Rules of the Narrative Genre(s)

Enter the narrative world these stories create, but discern the rules they have set. In other words, you have to look for the signs and directions the text leaves for us. Let me explain.

Genre is a technical term for intellectual work we do constantly throughout our days. For instance, if you pick up a book that begins with, "Once upon a time . . . ," you will immediately be able to make a number of conclusions about this piece of writing. You can assume that the story is a fairy tale, that it is aimed at a child's imagination, that it may invoke dragons and other mythical features, that it may involve intrigue and adventure, and that it will likely conclude with a moral of some sort. And all this you can discern with a mere four words. Those four words set the rules for how you read this text, for the kind of imagination the narrative demands in order to be heard. This is a different imagination than you might need when reading a newspaper article, an autobiography, or even a book like the one you are holding right now.

So also, biblical narratives are part of literary traditions or groupings. These narratives are not wholly unique, for they share with other texts of antiquity a certain set of reader expectations and rules for communicating. Part of your task in biblical studies, therefore, is not just comparing the narrative worlds of various biblical texts but also comparing these biblical texts with other texts of the ancient world that help us understand their genres.

Now, discerning the genre of a particular text is not just a trivial matter, not just an easy multiple-choice response. Instead, discerning the genre of a particular text means approaching that text expecting a particular way to teach and see the world. For instance, if we presume that the first few chapters of Genesis are a scientific, blow-by-blow account of the dawn of the universe as we know it, we might misread the meaning, purpose, and theological vision of Genesis. If we don't discern that Genesis is participating in a wider universe of cosmogonies (a fancy word for stories about the beginning of the world as we know it) including stories like the Enuma Elish and the Ba'al Epic, then we might read this text at cross-purposes, demanding answers for questions the text is not asking. After all, when we discern the genre of Genesis, we can also discern that its primary concern is not an outlining of the precise steps of creation but the character of the God responsible for them. Genesis, if we discern it correctly, is not about the world God creates so much as the kind of God that creates this kind of world.

We discern these rules of genre through study certainly but also by listening to the witness of others, by noting how others have heard God speaking through these texts. And there, the Spirit is most powerfully present.

3. Narratives Are Not Just Scripts for Our Lives

How then do these biblical narratives shape our lives today? Often, our first move is to seek to imitate the characters in these texts as exemplars of faithfulness. There is a reason why so many clothes emblazoned with WWJD (What Would Jesus Do?) sold so well for so long. You can't get much better shorthand for a life of faithfulness than to imagine what Jesus would do and then do it. Like Jesus, we ought to seek the lowly, embrace the poor, love the marginalized. Like Jesus, our circles should include people others would deem "sinners"—that is, those we might dare assume are unworthy of our company.

But imitation does not exhaust the power of narratives. Biblical narratives are not just scripts for our lives. We can turn to the book of Acts for a great example of what I mean. In the churches in which I grew up, Acts was typically treated as a manual for church thriving. That is, Acts was conceived as a portrait of a church that had their act together, a church that truly knew what it meant to be church. If we could go just go back to the way Acts did church, we would be much closer to the church God wants us to be. That is all well and good. Yes, in many ways, the early church in Acts is exemplary and worthy of imitation. After all, this was a community where believers sold their possessions and shared what they had so that no one lacked for anything Acts (4:32–37)!

And there we begin to see one problem with this approach. We tend to be selective about which elements of these narratives we want to imitate. Love your sisters and brothers in the church, sure, but sell my possessions? Not so much. Another reason we may hesitate to imitate the characters and situations we find in these narratives is that some of them are distressing or troubling. Should we imitate Ananias and Sapphira as they held back the proceeds from some property they sold, lying to their sisters and brothers and bringing upon themselves death (Acts 5:1–11)? Clearly not. But should we imitate the kind of harsh punishment inflicted upon them as they lie dead on the ground? Clearly not. What then is this story about? Perhaps it is about the high stakes involved in the relationships among those who gather together to worship God and care for one another. Perhaps it is a story that teaches that how we relate to one another is a matter of life and death to God. Perhaps it is an awakening in us of a particular kind of imagination by asking us to look closely at this terrible moment.

Narratives, then, we would suggest, are more about imagination than imitation. These stories help us imagine not just the particular world of Jesus' day or the earliest struggles of the church but new possibilities in our world. They help us imagine not just what *was* and *is* but what *could be*. They are about our present and future as much as they are about the past.

That is, what if these narratives inspired a renewed imagination for a world claimed by God, imbued with God's grace even as we struggle against sin's encroachments? After all, I may never meet a despised tax collector, but the stories in the Gospels about these marginalized people might open my eyes to modern-day "sinners" who I would rather not see, who I would rather exclude from my table and my life.

4. Give Room for Delight, for Narrative Is Art

Last, as we discussed above, we tell stories at least partly because stories are so delightful, because they entertain us. Stories can make us laugh and cry all at the same time. So also are the stories of Scripture. I wonder sometimes if we assume that the Bible has to be serious all the time, that reading Scripture is a sober activity of the deliberate and the stodgy. Nothing could be further from the truth. Scripture is entertaining. The end of the book of Acts is full of shipwrecks and adventures, for example. Scripture is delightful. The Gospels are full of stories we can't forget. Scripture is funny. Do you remember the story in Acts 20:7–12 when Paul preaches such a boring sermon that a young man falls out a window? That is funny! It's supposed to be funny. But because we tend to read these texts in ecclesial contexts that (rightly) feel weighty and serious, we forget to giggle when a young man's ennui pushes him out a window.

This is all to say that reading these stories is serious and delightful work. Reading these stories is troubling and insightful. Reading these stories is moving because in them God is still speaking in the way we most yearn for: stories, vibrant and beautiful stories.

 **Notes**

1. See Greg Carey, *Sinners: Jesus and His Earliest Followers* (Waco, TX: Baylor University Press, 2009).

2. See Phyllis Trible, *Texts of Terror: Literary-Feminist Readings of Biblical Narratives* (Minneapolis, MN: Fortress Press, 1984).

Chapter 14

How Do We Read
Four Gospels?

The Bible canonizes difference. As we have argued throughout this book, the Bible is a collection of voices, a library of texts. These voices and texts speak from different places and times. Sometimes they voice similar questions, but even those echoed queries are distinctive in their own way. Sometimes they voice similar responses, but just as often theological conclusions are tested and reoriented as the people of God are tried and turned around.

The Bible canonizes difference, and this is perhaps that much more evident at the very front of the New Testament. In telling the stories of the ministry, teaching, death, and resurrection of Jesus, we have four distinct portraits. Each of the Gospels tell these stories in distinct ways, in ways not easily harmonized with the other three. At the very beginning of the New Testament, we have *four* stories about Jesus, not one, even if we have managed to harmonize those stories in our own minds.

Let's explore these four portraits of Jesus by taking a closer look at one example. In all four Gospels, Jesus has a meal at someone's home. During that meal, a woman finds her way to Jesus and gives him a gift. Someone, however, is appalled, noting that the woman has no place at this table. Jesus contradicts him. These are the broad parameters of the story. The details in the four Gospels reveal how complex, well-constructed, and theologically distinct these stories are. Take a look at them.

Matt. 26:6   Now while Jesus was at Bethany in the house of Simon the leper, [7] a woman came to him with an alabaster jar of very costly ointment, and she poured it on his head as he sat at the table. [8] But when the disciples saw it, they were angry and said, "Why this waste? [9] For this ointment could have been sold for a large sum, and the money given to the poor." [10] But Jesus, aware of this, said to them, "Why do you trouble the woman? She has performed a good service for me. [11] For you always have the poor with you, but you will not always have me. [12] By pouring this ointment on my body she has prepared me for burial. [13] Truly I tell you, wherever this good news is proclaimed in the whole world, what she has done will be told in remembrance of her."

Mark 14:3   While he was at Bethany in the house of Simon the leper, as he sat at the table, a woman came with an alabaster jar of very costly ointment of nard, and she broke open the jar and poured the ointment on his head. [4] But some were there who said to one another in anger, "Why was the ointment wasted in this way? [5] For this ointment could have been sold for more than three hundred denarii, and the money given to the poor." And they scolded her. [6] But Jesus said, "Let her alone; why do you trouble her? She has performed a good service for me. [7] For you always have the poor with you, and you can show kindness to them whenever you wish; but you will not always have me. [8] She has done what she could; she has anointed my body beforehand for its burial. [9] Truly I tell you, wherever the good news is proclaimed in the whole world, what she has done will be told in remembrance of her."

Luke 7:36   One of the Pharisees asked Jesus to eat with him, and he went into the Pharisee's house and took his place at the table. [37] And a woman in the city, who was a sinner, having learned that he was eating in the Pharisee's house, brought an alabaster jar of ointment. [38] She stood behind him at his feet, weeping, and began to bathe his feet with her tears and to dry them with her hair. Then she continued kissing his feet and anointing them with the ointment. [39] Now when the Pharisee who had invited him saw it, he said to himself, "If this man were a prophet, he would have known who and what kind of woman this is who is touching him—that she is a sinner." [40] Jesus spoke up and said to him, "Simon, I have something to say to you." "Teacher," he replied, "Speak." [41] "A certain creditor had two debtors; one owed five hundred denarii, and the other fifty. [42] When they could not pay, he canceled the debts for both of them. Now which of them will love him more?" [43] Simon answered, "I suppose the one for whom he canceled the greater debt." And Jesus said to him, "You have judged rightly." [44] Then turning toward the woman, he said to Simon, "Do you see this woman? I entered your house; you gave me no water for my feet, but she has bathed my feet with her tears and dried them with her hair. [45] You gave me no kiss, but from the time I came in she has not stopped kissing my feet. [46] You did not anoint my head with oil, but she has anointed my feet with ointment. [47] Therefore, I tell you, her sins, which were many, have been forgiven; hence she has shown great love. But the one to whom little is forgiven, loves little." [48] Then he said to her, "Your sins are forgiven." 49But those who were at the table with him began to say among themselves, "Who is this who even forgives sins?" [50] And he said to the woman, "Your faith has saved you; go in peace."

John 12:1   Six days before the Passover Jesus came to Bethany, the home of Lazarus, whom he had raised from the dead. [2] There they gave a dinner for him. Martha served, and Lazarus was one of those at the table with him. [3] Mary took a pound of costly perfume made of pure nard, anointed Jesus' feet, and wiped them with her hair. The house was filled with the fragrance of the perfume. [4] But Judas Iscariot, one of his disciples (the one who was about to betray him), said, [5] "Why was this perfume not sold for three hundred denarii and the money given to the poor?" [6] (He said this not because he cared about the poor, but because he was a thief; he kept the common purse and used to steal what was put into it.) [7] Jesus said, "Leave her alone. She bought it so that she might keep it for the day of my burial. [8] You always have the poor with you, but you do not always have me."

Notice some of the differences among the four stories. Matthew, Mark, and John agree that this story occurs in Bethany while Luke does not indicate where the story occurs. In Matthew and Mark, the host is a certain Simon the leper—that is, Jesus' dining with Simon in these two accounts would raise the ire of Jesus' critics. However, in Luke, Simon is not a leper but a Pharisee who has invited Jesus into his home, much better company than a leper in the eyes of most. In John, the hosts are Martha and Lazarus, who was raised from the dead earlier in John's narrative. Matthew, Mark, and Luke agree that an unnamed woman arrives with an "alabaster jar of ointment." In Matthew and Mark, she is not identified by name though in Luke she is called a "sinner." In Matthew and Mark, she anoints Jesus' head, but in Luke and John it is his feet that receive the benefit of this treatment. In all four stories, someone objects to this extravagant act. In Matthew, the disciples grumble. In Mark, "some [who] were there" are upset. In Luke, Simon complains to himself; Jesus can read his mind or perhaps just the expression on his face. In John, it is Judas who protests. In Matthew, Mark, and John, the complaint is similar: pouring out such expensive ointment is a waste, for it could have been sold and the proceeds given to the poor. Luke is alone in recording Simon's protestations that were Jesus a true prophet, he would have known what kind of woman was touching him. When Jesus responds in Matthew, Mark, and John, he chides the critics of this woman, noting that this anointing was preparing him for his burial. In Luke, Jesus says nothing about his burial, instead narrating a parable about forgiveness. The stories conclude differently too. Matthew and Mark have Jesus commending the woman and saying that her good deed would be long remembered. Luke's Jesus forgives the woman of her sins and sends her out in peace.

And yet perhaps the most significant difference is not *what* happens in these stories but *when*. Matthew, Mark, and John all set this story near the end of Jesus ministry, a prelude to the cross. In Luke, however, the story comes rather early in the narrative, far away from Holy Week.

So which story is right? True? Best? This is an ancient problem, as old as some of the earliest readers of these texts.

These four stories pose a problem for us. But what kind of problem? For some readers of the Gospels, the problem is primarily historical. Some readers want to know what really happened in Jesus' life. Did he cleanse the temple and cast out the moneychangers at the beginning of his ministry like John suggests or at the end of his ministry, as Matthew, Mark, and Luke narrate? Was Jesus visited by shepherds, magi, or both after he was born? Did Jesus preach a powerful sermon on a hill or on a plain? Did he say, "Blessed are the poor" or "Blessed are the poor in spirit"? Or did he say, "Blessed are the cheesemakers," as the writers of the movie *The Life of Brian* suggested some might have misheard? What were Jesus' words from the cross? Did Judas commit suicide by hanging himself on a tree, or did he fall forward and find himself disemboweled? From a certain historical perspective, only one story out of these many versions was truly possible, and so one of the most important—if not *the* most important—tasks we have as readers is discerning which passages are authentic and which are fictions. Who was the historical Jesus?

And yet that seems insufficient to us at some level. Such questions are important, but they don't exhaust what these texts might mean for us today. After all, the ancient authors of these texts are not after comprehensive, chronologically precise narrations of Jesus' days. These are not objective biographies meant to deliver the facts of Jesus' life. These are *believers* writing and editing these stories. The authors of these Gospels are not just curious about Jesus' life for curiosity's sake. Instead, the Gospel writers have found that they and their communities have been transformed by an encounter with the living Jesus! That is, they are deeply implicated in the stories they are sharing. They are deeply interested in how the story is told and how its telling will affect others. They are writing less to record these events in order to preserve a particular chronology and more to understand who this Jesus is by narrating a compelling, truthful story. And they want to understand this not so much by tracing Jesus' comings and goings but by catching a glimpse of how God was working through his life, death, and resurrection. That is, the historical questions are important but not ultimate. They provide important vistas into the life of Jesus, but they do not exhaust the meaning of these stories.

Think about it this way: would you be willing to trade the four Gospels for unedited, uncut, multicamera footage of Jesus' life, ministry, death, and resurrection? That is, is a comprehensive and real-time record of Jesus preferable to what we have now, four distinct accounts that resist harmonization? After years of study of these texts, we, the authors, would reject that trade. We seek not the "historical" Jesus so much as the "real" Jesus who has encountered us in our faith.[1] We don't seek a Jesus captured pristinely and perfectly on film. We seek the Jesus who has transformed someone's life so much so that she is compelled to write this story down for the sake of her neighbors. We seek the Jesus who confounds us and comforts us, frustrates us and fulfills us. In these four inspired narratives, we think we catch a fuller glimpse into who Jesus was and is than we would with a single, supposedly definitive account. Most importantly, these four stories bear witness to the significance and meaning of this ancient Jesus who is still preaching, still healing, still living but never dying. As Baptist theologian Walter Shurden once noted, "The Gospels are portraits, not photographs of Jesus."[2]

Therefore, the problem we face in reading *four* Gospels is not a quest to sift the authentic Jesus from the inauthentic one. The problem we face is that all four portraits are truthful, *and* they are distinct. All four portraits are faithful accounts of the significance of Jesus' life for those who seek to follow his ways, *and* they each tell a different story about Jesus. All four portraits are needed, for no single story could possible encapsulate or capture or contain a story that can speaks word of life in our midst. At the same time, these four Gospels resist our efforts to harmonize them. These four Gospels and the church's decision long ago to embrace all four in all their particularity is a canonizing of difference that reminds us that God speaks in many ways still today.

In short, the problem for us—for those of us called to proclaim these stories as word of God, for those of us compelled to follow Jesus of Nazareth—is *theological*. How is it that God's Word speaks through these four rather different stories of Jesus? How is it that Jesus' story is most faithfully told through a fourfold Gospel? And to what kind of God do these four narratives bear witness?

Fortunately, this is not a new question. We are heirs of deep theological reflection on these questions, even in the earliest days of those communities that sought to follow Jesus. Let me introduce you to a few examples from the early church.

According to church tradition, Papias was the bishop of Hierapolis from approximately 70 to 136 CE. He may have had connections to the apostle John and to other leaders in the early church. We have fragments of his writings thanks to the work of the church chronicler Eusebius, including the following:

> I will not hesitate to add also for you to my interpretations what I formerly learned with care from the Presbyters and

have carefully stored in memory, giving assurance of its truth. For I did not take pleasure as the many do in those who speak much, but in those who teach what is true, nor in those who relate foreign precepts, but in those who relate the precepts which were given by the Lord to the faith and came down from the Truth itself. And also if any follower of the Presbyters happened to come, I would inquire for the sayings of the Presbyters, what Andrew said, or what Peter said, or what Philip or what Thomas or James or what John or Matthew or any other of the Lord's disciples, and for the things which other of the Lord's disciples, and for the things which Ariston and the Presbyter John, the disciples of the Lord, were saying. For I considered that I should not get so much advantage from matter in books as from the voice which yet lives and remains.

This is a fascinating glimpse into early contests among followers of Jesus. In a time before the canon was closed, in a time when many Gospel accounts were likely circulating among the churches, Papias warns his readers/hearers to be careful. Papias seems more comfortable with a living tradition shared from person to person rather than written texts. The former, in his mind, is more reliable, for it preserves our connection with the past. And by reliable here he doesn't just mean historically accurate as we tend to assume but theologically truthful. Is the Jesus portrayed in these various accounts true to the God we seek to follow? So, in these early days, texts were not necessarily trusted by all, for they could be forged. They could be full of error. On the other hand, there was the living word, a word that was carried from disciple to follower of Jesus. Such a word could be trusted more.

We could also turn to the writings of Irenaeus of Lyons, a bishop who lived from about 140 to 202 CE. In his *Against Heresies*, he writes, "There are four gospels and only four, neither more nor less: four like the points of the compass, four like the chief directions of the wind. The Church, spread all over the world, has in the gospels four pillars and four winds blowing wherever people live. These four gospels are in actual fact one single Gospel, a fourfold Gospel inspired by the one Spirit, a Gospel which has four aspects representing the work of the Son of God."[3] That is, quite early on, Christians were grappling with this question of four Gospels. For Irenaeus, the four Gospels might be distinct, but they also are unified in their Christology and theology. All four were needed to sustain the church.

But this wasn't the only approach taken in the early church. Tatian, a second-century Christian thinker, composed a text called the *Diatessaron*. That name is made up of two Greek words: *dia,* which means "through," and *tessa,* which means "four." The Diatessaron created an extended harmony of the four Gospels. It includes every story found in the four Gospels and aligns them in what Tatian believed was a chronological order. So, for instance, Jesus cleanses the temple at the beginning of his ministry as in John *and* at the end of his ministry as he does according to Matthew, Mark, and Luke.

So which is the better solution to the "problem" of four Gospels? For much of the church, Irenaeus won the day. In our Bibles, we don't have one Gospel but four, not a Diatessaron but a fourfold Gospel.

There is one more source we might consider, and it comes from the Gospel of Luke itself. The Gospels opens with the following: "Since many have undertaken to set down an orderly account of the events that have been fulfilled among us, just as they were handed on to us by those who from the beginning were eyewitnesses and servants of the word, I too decided, after investigating everything carefully from the very first, to write an orderly account for you, most excellent Theophilus, so that you may know the truth concerning the things about which you have been instructed" (Luke 1:1–4).

In my classes, I often spend a whole class session dissecting just these four verses. There are such treasures for students of the Gospels in this brief text. Notice, for instance, that Luke acknowledges that he is not the first to write a Gospel. "Many have undertaken" this work, he acknowledges. But why then add his voice to these other witnesses? He writes, "So that you may know the truth concerning the things about which you have been instructed." This is a text primarily for those who already believe, not as much for people who don't know this story. No one needs a spoiler alert when Jesus starts predicting his death and resurrection. No one is surprised when the tomb is empty three days later. What matters for Luke is not *that* he tells the story but *how* and *why* he tells the story. He tells the story, shapes the narrative to confirm and affirm those believers who hear his account. And how does he do this? By telling an "orderly account." Here, he doesn't mean that he laid the story out in precise chronological order but that he arranges a story that is theologically compelling and convincing.

Remember, his aim isn't to tell the story for the first time but to help those who know the story of Jesus know it in an even more "truthful" way.

Even in the Bible itself, the function of these four Gospels is a vital question pulsating at the very center of the stories we tell about Jesus. How do we tell the story of Jesus when we have four stories of Jesus that are not entirely at odds but not unanimous either?

For those of us called into the work of Christian ministry, the "solution" to the "problem" of four Gospels is theological primarily. What kind of God is being portrayed in these stories? How do the similarities and tensions between these portraits help elucidate the character of God? But the "solution" is also literary. That is, what is the relationship between these texts? And how does understanding these relationships clarify how to read these texts? If we are convinced that Mark was written earliest, that Matthew and Luke both draw upon Mark and perhaps a common source along with independent sources, that John seems to be writing with a different stream of traditions about Jesus, then how do we read each text?

And perhaps "solution" is the wrong word for how we seek to resolve this theological problem. For, in the end, the aim of the reader of four Gospels is not to harmonize these stories or to forward one account as authentic while rejecting the others. Neither is it to avoid taking seriously the distinctive testimony of each Gospel. Our aim is to listen to the voice of the God Jesus followed in these Gospels. In the case of the Gospels, we hear God speaking most clearly in a diversity of accounts, in the multiplicity of perspectives they bear.

◎⊙ Notes

1. See Luke Timothy Johnson, *The Real Jesus? The Misguided Quest for the Historical Jesus and the Truth of the Traditional Gospels* (New York: HarperOne, 1996).

2. Walter B. Shurden, *The Baptist Identity: Four Fragile Freedoms* (Macon, GA: Smyth & Helwys, 1993), 17.

3. Irenaeus, *Against Heresies* 3.11.8.

Chapter 15

How Do We Read the
Letters of Paul?

aul's letters were not written to us. And yet Paul's letters were written to us. Confused? Let's explain.

In the middle of the New Testament are thirteen letters written by or purported to be written by Paul. These letters have been interpreted and contested since they were first received. So much ink has been spilled considering the meaning of these texts, especially the effort to understand the doctrinal convictions Paul was propounding. In Paul's letters, generations of Christians have sought to understand the meaning of the cross and the resurrection. We have sought to know something about law and grace and gospel and sin and life and death. And we have disagreed—often vehemently—about what Paul had to say then and what Paul still has to say to us today.

And so the legacy of Paul and the Pauline letters is important *and* complex. For some readers, Paul is a faithful guide to the most important questions of theology we might broach. In the Pauline letters, we have a sure, even comprehensive accounting of theology and Christology.

But for others, Paul's legacy is more problematic. Pauline letters have been cited as evidence to sanction slavery and to keep women from ordination and leadership in the church. For our gay and lesbian sisters and brothers, the opening chapter of Romans has been used to sanction their exclusion from God's grace, even their demonization as being beyond the salvation God offers us freely.

So what do we make of these letters? How do we read them in faithful and imaginative ways that pay attention to their complex legacies? How do we preach and teach Paul's words alongside Jesus' teachings? What do we make of texts that have clarified so much yet also hurt so many? In short, how can a letter written a long, long time ago for a people very, very different than us be a word of God for us today? And how can our interpretations confront directly the heights and depths of those interpreters who have gone before us?

At least, we start by acknowledging that these letters were *not* written to us. That is, we are not the intended or original recipients of these correspondences. In a very real way, we are reading someone else's mail. My name was not on the "envelope." Instead, it was the various communities of believers dotting the Mediterranean landscape in the first century who first received these letters. It was their names that were on Paul's lips as he prayed for them. It was their questions and joys and anxieties that compelled Paul to write. Whether Paul wrote with encouragement or disappointment, it was not *our* lives that precipitated his words. It was the distinctive, particular, unique people and situations of these early churches that stirred Paul's heart and voice.

Reading someone else's mail comes with a plethora of limitations. For instance, we are not privy to the other side of the correspondence. We cannot know fully what the Romans or Corinthians or Galatians asked of Paul or how they responded to his letters. Every once in a while Paul gives us a glimpse into what these communities might have asked of him or the local crises that were stirring up questions (e.g., 1 Thess. 4:13). But even such glimpses into these communities are fleeting and shaped by Paul's perceptions. It proves difficult if not impossible to re-create exactly what was going on in these communities. And so reading Paul's letters can sometimes feel like hearing one side of a phone conversation. We can hear what Paul was saying, though the voices of the communities to which he wrote are muffled and distant.

The difficulties are even more extensive when we remember the cultural and historical gaps that yawn between the communities that first read these letters and our own time. Our contexts are not those of the Thessalonians or the community that worshiped in Philemon's home. Theirs is a world where very different assumptions about the world and humanity were held. So even if we could reconstruct or discover what the Corinthians wrote to

Paul (see 2 Cor. 2:4), we would still face a massive cultural gap between them and us.

These letters were not written to us. They were not written to answer our questions or anxieties or hopes. They were written to people whose experiences we can seek to reconstruct but will always be beyond our full comprehension.

And yet these *are* letters written to us. As followers of Jesus, we confess that these texts are not just errant letters upon which we happened to stumble but the very word of God. Though some of our ancestors in the faith may have failed to read these texts as life-giving words from a God of grace and judgment, these texts have led other communities into the mysteries of God's love for the whole of creation. These *are* letters written to us because through them and their interpretation in communities of faith we hear God's voice speaking.

A few key questions will help us get started in thinking about how we might listen to that divine voice.

Who Wrote Paul's Letters?

We are asking this question in two different ways. First, we are wondering whether Paul or someone else claiming to be Paul wrote the thirteen letters that bear his name in the New Testament. Scholars tend to agree that seven of the letters are clearly authentic: Romans, 1 and 2 Corinthians, Galatians, Philippians, 1 Thessalonians, and Philemon. Meanwhile, the authenticity of the other Pauline letters (Ephesians, Colossians, 2 Thessalonians, 1 and 2 Timothy, and Titus) is frequently questioned. Conclusions about the authorship of these letters are not universal, of course. A number of scholars will question this conclusion. Some will want to include more letters in the list of authentic Pauline letters. Some will want to contend that all thirteen are authentically Pauline. Such disputes will only continue. Your task as a reader of these texts is not just to determine which of these letters you think were written by Paul so you can ignore the rest. Instead, your engagement with authorship should shift *how,* not *whether* you read these texts. So, for instance, if you conclude that 1 Timothy was written by someone other than Paul, such a conclusion should shape how you read the letter's admonition to reserve leadership of faith communities exclusively to the men of that community (1 Tim. 2:11–12).

But there is another layer to the question we wish to explore. The question also refers to the person or persons who actually wrote the text down, even if she or he would not be technically the author of the text. It was Paul's practice to write using an amanuensis or secretary. Paul would dictate his letters aloud, and the amanuensis would write down Paul's words as he spoke. There is evidence of this in Paul's letters themselves. Note, for instance, Gal. 6:11: "See what large letters I make when I am writing in my own hand!" Likely, Paul stopped dictating at this very moment, and borrowing the scribe's writing tool, he used his own hand to write this line in larger letters than the rest of the text. (As a side note, we would love to see a Bible actually print this verse in a larger font.) Or see Philemon 19 when Paul again takes up the writing of the letter with his own hand: "I, Paul, am writing this with my own hand: I will repay it I say nothing about your owing me even your own self." At this critical and personal moment in this tense letter, Paul takes over from his secretary to plead and cajole Philemon with his own handwriting.

What might this mean for how we interpret Paul's letters? Well, we ought not imagine Paul's amanuensis as an ancient version of Siri or Alexa, dutifully writing down all Paul said, mistakes and "ums" and all. Nor should we imagine a court stenographer recording precisely exactly what was said. Instead, imagine a secretary who might edit on the fly if Paul made a grammatical mistake or might even ask Paul to restate and clarify again what he had said. That is, this secretary might be an editor as much as she or he is a stenographer.

In a sense then, Paul's letters were not just the works of singular genius, writing away in solitude in his study. Instead, we have here documents that speak about relationships, imagine new ways of relating to one another, but also practice a kind of relational composition. And perhaps this is true in another way as well.

Who Read Paul's Letters?

This question is also a bit ambiguous. What we mean here primarily is not just those first audiences that received these letters. These communities in their rich cultural and theological contexts would have read these letters quite differently than we do these many years hence. And as we noted above, reconstructing fully how they would have read these letters is beyond our abilities, to be sure.

But we also want to point to yet another act of interpretation present in the reading of these letters in their ancient contexts. Remember that there were no copy machines in the ancient world, no e-mail correspondence by which to share Paul's missives. There was no postal service to deliver them. Instead, Paul entrusted individuals not just to carry these letters to their addresses but also to be the first to read them. The carrier of the letter most likely also read these letters aloud to these ancient audiences in the house churches where they worshiped and shared a holy meal. Now, imagine hearing the letter to the Romans or even the letter to Philemon and the church that met in his house. Imagine hearing these letters for the first time. Imagine how many questions would have emerged from the very first. What did Paul mean when he talked about sin and death? What does Paul want us to do with Onesimus? And the questions would continue.

And who was there to answer these questions? Not Paul but the carrier of his letters. Now, the following is something one of us learned from one of our teachers, Beverly Gaventa. If such a carrier would be responsible for answering these important questions about these important letters, wouldn't it seem likely that the carrier might be involved in writing the letter in the first place? Might that carrier have been in the room when Paul was composing and rewriting? Might the letters have been the product not of Paul alone or even Paul and his secretary but Paul and those he trusted most to explain and interpret what he wrote to these communities? If this is so, then notice who carried and read Paul's letter to the Romans, that letter that has caused so much theological and scholarly consternation about its meaning then and its meaning now. Who carried and read and interpreted this letter for the first time?

None other than a woman named Phoebe (see Rom. 16:1–2). Knowing these realities just might influence how we read these letters. It might remind us that these letters were oral performances before they were texts. It might remind us that they were shaped by many human hands. It might remind us that it was through these frail humans that God spoke then and is still speaking today.

How Do We Read Paul's Letters?

We could say much, much more about how we read Paul's letters, but this is but a brief introduction to these complex correspondences. In my classes,

I often share these four guidelines for reading Paul as some initial steps in this interpretive journey.

1. What is the "therefore" there for?

    You will notice a number of conjunctions in Paul's letters: and, but, for, therefore, so. These little words are reminders that Paul constructs complex but connected sets of arguments in his letters. So reading, for instance, the beginning of Romans 8 ("There is *therefore* now no condemnation for those who are in Christ Jesus") should lead us to ask what the "therefore" is there for. To what is Paul pointing for us to comprehend this powerful confession of God's forgiveness of our sins? What we'll discover is that Paul is pointing to seven chapters of argumentation that culminate here at the beginning of chapter 8 but continue through the end of the letter. It is not enough to read Rom. 8:1, as powerful as it is. The "therefore" should drive us to know the road by which Paul arrives at this conclusion. And that road starts not at the beginning of chapter 8 but the very beginning of the letter.

2. Context is key.

    As noted earlier in this chapter, these letters were written to specific people in specific places at a specific time. So, knowing something about these people, places, and times is needed in our study of Paul. We can turn to the closing chapters of Paul's letters, where we find lists of individuals he greets. What can we learn from these names about the kinds of communities Paul was addressing? We can turn to historical, archeological, and sociological analyses of these ancient cities. What was it like to live in the city of Rome in the first century? What would one's daily realities be at the center of this imperial city?

3. Paul's letters are occasional.

    Paul's letters are all precipitated by a particular occasion. Paul is not thinking abstractly about questions of doctrine so much as addressing the pressing concerns of these communities. Paul writes 1 Thessalonians not so much to write a doctrine of eschatology or the end but to encourage the believers in this city who were grieving that their loved ones who had died might miss the imminent resurrection Jesus had promised. If they were in the ground already, could God bring them back, they wondered? This was not a question of abstract theology but a pulsing, existential anxiety at the heart of their faith. Discerning what occasions led Paul to write will help us recall the embodied faith that Paul is addressing.

4. Read, read, and reread.

Most important of all is this: read, read, and reread. Read with others in your community of faith. Read with others who see the world very differently than you do. Read and read and reread because these letters cannot be exhausted in a single sitting. There is always more to learn from Paul and those with whom we read these ancient letters.

So, what might God be telling us after all these years when we turn to Paul's letters? Frequently, we might assume that the essence of Paul's letters are the ideas found therein, that the doctrines and beliefs Paul propounds linger over the years as the most important part of these ancient letters. We sometimes assume that the way to bridge the cultural and historical gaps between our time and Paul's time is to focus on what he might teach us about Christology, eschatology, and theology.

To be sure, there is much to learn about such significant theological insights. But to focus on Paul's *ideas* and neglect that these ideas were directed at living, breathing communities will mean we miss a critical part of how God might speaking through Paul's letters.

In the end, Paul's letters are not about ideas so much as the many ways God has brought strangers into each other's orbits, how God's forgiveness makes siblings of us all. That is, Paul's letters are not really about getting our doctrine right about God, about saying the right things about God. Instead, Paul's letters point us to a God who draws us together still. In a world full of so much division, this is good news indeed.

Chapter 16

How Do We Read Apocalyptic Literature?

Apocalypse Then and Now

The words *apocalypse* and *apocalyptic* are strikingly common in our culture. Groups claiming the imminent end of the world rise (and fall) all the time. Do a Google Images search of these terms, and you will find a stunning array of pictures depicting mayhem, dystopia, and of course zombies. Lots and lots of zombies. Evidence of the dawning age of the undead can be found on everything from video games to ammunition boxes.

The Bible has apocalyptic ideas too. They are found in Daniel 7–12 and Revelation, most notably. So how do modern understandings of the apocalypse compare to the ancient understandings found in the Bible?

Let's begin with a few definitions. First, when biblical scholars refer to "apocalypse," they are not talking about a grim and gloomy event of global destruction but rather a particular literary genre. For scholars, an "apocalypse" is:

> a genre of revelatory literature with a narrative framework, in which a revelation is mediated by an otherworldly being to a human recipient, disclosing a transcendent reality which is both temporal, insofar as it envisages eschatological salvation, and spatial insofar as it involves another, supernatural world.[1]

Admittedly, this definition is just about as dense and mysterious as the visions it tries to describe. So let's do a bit of unpacking.

To say that apocalypses are revelatory is to say that they unveil mysteries, truths, and realities in the "spiritual realm." In fact, the term *apocalypse* in Greek means unveiling, disclosure, or revelation (cf. Rev. 1:1). Apocalypses assume that the cosmos is made up of two realities: the "empirical" world that can be perceived through the senses and the unseen world of God, angels, and other hidden forces. These two worlds interact with one another in a variety of ways, and one function of apocalypses is to reveal how, when, and where those interactions take place. That is, apocalyptic literature *narrates* or tells a story about the encounter of the otherworldly we can't see and the worldly we can. In that interaction, God and/or God's agents disclose some profound truth we would have otherwise not been able to know.

Daniel 7 is an excellent example of an apocalypse. It begins in the same way many other narratives do—with a chronological notice: "In the first year of King Belshazzar of Babylon, Daniel had a dream and visions of his head as he lay in bed" (Dan. 7:1). What Daniel sees in the night is bizarre and troubling, not only to us but also to him (Dan. 7:15). The chapter begins by narrating what Daniel saw (Dan. 7:1–14), followed by an interpretation of these strange dreams (Dan. 7:15–28). The effect of the chapter's structure is that we the readers, like Daniel, are left to ponder the meaning of these visions until Daniel finally approaches one of YHWH's attendants to ask for an interpretation (Dan. 7:16–18).

We learn in verses 16 through 18 that the four beasts represent "four kings" who "shall arise out of the earth." Despite their terrible might, "the holy ones of the Most High shall receive the kingdom and possess the kingdom forever—forever and ever" (Dan. 7:18). Like other apocalypses, Daniel 7 is fundamentally political; it is about power. But the hidden power that allows these kings to exist and persist is the enthroned "Ancient of Days." For the book of Daniel, *all* earthly power is granted and revoked by God alone (vv. 11–12; cf. Dan. 2:20–23). Even the most terrifying and boastful earthly powers are finally subject to the king over all kings.

The closing book of the Bible, Revelation, is also clearly apocalyptic. It narrates how John finds himself transported into the heavenly throne room of God while he is exiled on the island of Patmos. In this heavenly journey, he catches glimpses of dragons and beasts and warfare and deliverance. Also, John narrates how the faithful will be delivered from powers represented by those dragons and monsters. In the end, he sees a new Jerusalem descending from the heavens and planted on a re-created earth. That city becomes the home of the faithful, shielded from death and oppression and constantly accompanied by God's presence. Revelation, like Daniel, is full of symbolic language because the genre of the apocalyptic demands it but more importantly because the truths are such that only powerful symbols can capture them. Symbolic language may be one way to critique safely the current powers of John's time (in his case, the Roman Empire); if a Roman official found Revelation, would he realize that the text is calling for or envisioning the empire's downfall? But more than that, symbolic language may capture truths so profound that mere descriptive language cannot contain them.

These two texts in particular have inspired a great deal of speculation about their meaning. From movies to books and conspiratorial websites, some have sought to unlock the mysteries of these texts. Such readings have treated these texts like puzzles that need to be solved, codes that with the right cypher will show us precisely what the future holds. This is a profound misreading of such literature. Let's focus on a few basics.

1. First, apocalyptic literature is not abstract reflection about some unseen future but a word of encouragement or a word of warning to the communities they address. That is, when we imagine the authors of Daniel and Revelation, we ought not picture a psychic gazing into a cloudy orb to read our futures. These are not just hazy visions about some distant future but concrete declarations about the character of God in profoundly troubling times.

2. Second then, these texts were probably decipherable to their first audiences. The symbols and referents of these books might be confounding to us, but this may have more to do with our cultural and historical distance from these events rather than the obscurity of these texts. After all, why would these texts have been written, interpreted, shared, and transmitted throughout time if they were not significant to those who read and found in them God's word? That is, the author of these texts wrote not to confound but to comfort and confront.

3. Third, these texts are about the present as much as they are about the future. Apocalyptic texts are ways to imagine a faithful way of life in the midst of challenging moments. When the world seems to be collapsing, when all hope is lost, can we trust God's promises? Apocalyptic

literature says yes by pointing to God's promised future so that we can lean into that future with hope even as it seems distant.

4. So, fourth, apocalyptic literature is about faith and hope in the end, not fear or anxiety. These texts sought to empower their readers with faith, not paralyze them with anxiety. These texts declare that judgment is coming, that we too might be caught up in that judgment. And yet we can be sure of God's faithfulness, even in the midst of suffering. We can be certain that God will deliver us. Because of that hope, we need not see the world with fear but with a hope that is infused with God's promises.

Apocalyptic Literature Matters for Theology

We might be tempted to treat apocalyptic literature as a sedative in the midst of trouble, as escapist literature. Don't worry about the future. God will be victorious in the end! But these texts ought not function as a mere opiate for the masses. These texts do not provide us with an excuse to sit on our hands as we await the end. These texts can help us think about what is ultimately important. They can sharpen our vision, fill out our hopes, express our deepest fears, and finally affect how we live toward our neighbors in the present.

Here, the apostle Paul is most helpful. Now, Paul's letters aren't the first place many of us think about when we imagine apocalyptic literature, but his letters are tinged at important moments with an apocalyptic imagination, an imagination about what is possible in God's ultimate fulfilling of all of God's promises. Paul emphasizes repeatedly how important the community of faith is, how vital life lived together as sisters and brothers is. For Paul, then, musings on the end are not esoteric or merely otherworldly; instead, his thoughts on the end clarify what life *today* looks like. The future is in service of the present, not the other way around.

In the midst of a discussion about resurrection and God's deliverance of the faithful from death, Paul twice calls for these communities to "encourage one another" with the apocalyptic hopes he outlines (see 1 Thess. 4:18; 5:11). Paul here is explicit about the purpose of eschatological reflection. These theological reflections are not meant to sedate us in the midst of great tribulations. Nor are they meant to lead us to lives of passivity, wherein we twiddle our thumbs as we await the coming of Jesus. Instead, Paul twice makes clear that these words are meant for mutual encouragement.

Paul says, "Encourage one another with these words." Not inspire fear in one another. Not draw attention to your ability to pinpoint the very day of Christ's return. Not bludgeon one another with these words. Not neglect this teaching. But encourage one another!

In a sense, for Paul, these reflections on the end are about the present day. These reflections teach us not how to live *then* but how to live *now*. An apocalyptic imagination can therefore help us think about what is ultimately important.

For too long, too many Christians have ceded theological ground to fanciful eschatological dreamers who treat the living word of God as a mere puzzle to be solved, a complex cypher only the purportedly enlightened can decode. But apocalyptic literature is not about providing a road map to the end of days. Instead, these texts can be a radical way to shape how we relate to God and one another today. They outline a posture of trust in God and God's work. So these texts are not about bold predictions about days yet to come. They are about seeing the work of God in seemingly ordinary, unremarkable moments.

 Notes

1. See John J. Collins, *The Apocalyptic Imagination: An Introduction to Jewish Apocalyptic Literature,* 2nd ed. (Grand Rapids, MI: Eerdmans, 1998), 5.

Conclusion

We started this book by saying that we never read the Bible by ourselves. In short, we need each other to read the Bible. This is not something we can do alone.

We need teachers who will teach us the languages and histories and contexts that nurtured the texts we have called Scripture. We need preachers who will help us imagine how these texts speak to us still today. We need diverse neighbors to help us see what we have been missing all along. We need the wisdom of those who have been faithful for years and years. We need the fresh insight of those who are just now picking up these texts for the first time. We need one another.

But most of all we need God's inspiring presence in our midst. God took a risk in entrusting the gospel to human words and expression. Human words can fall short. Words can be misunderstood and twisted with ill intent. Our interpretations of these words can revive dry bones or oppress vulnerable neighbors. God took a risk in entrusting Scripture to human words and expression. We also take a risk when we encounter these words and allow them to change us.

The gospel is God's action of liberating us from the forces of sin and death. The gospel is God's completing of creation and the enlivening of our bodies. The gospel is the gift of true freedom, freedom from that sinful voice that would tell us we are not worthy of God's love or anyone else's, for that matter, freedom from the affliction of death that kills and takes and sickens.

But this freedom can never be about mere independence or isolation from our neighbors near and far. Freedom for the follower of Jesus rejects our comfort for the sake of welcoming the other. Freedom for the follower of Jesus is characterized by trust in the resurrection and thus vulnerability toward those we meet.

We lean into the resurrection power even as we yet live in a world full of death.

But sacred texts do not have arms that might wield a sword, fists that might strike the other, feet that might trample the small, hands that might pound the vulnerable. Sacred texts cannot act on their own. Sacred texts cannot do anything apart from readers and communities of interpretation. We might be tempted to see the supposedly inherent violence and imbedded oppression of religious traditions that aren't our own. But we who are followers of Christ would be casting stones in a glass house. After all, Western Christians in particular live in a glass house built on a foundation of imperialism, slavery, and genocide. But that foundation is even more complex. That foundation also includes spiritual giants who have beamed with hopeful light and anonymous believers who have been guided by God's Spirit to serve God and neighbor alike. That is, ours is a mottled history, tinged with violence and grace, oppression and freedom, nihilism and hopefulness.

And in every case the Bible has been used as sanction and warrant, whether for good or ill. In every case, these texts have been militated for and against the other. To be more precise, the text hasn't done any of these things, whether good or ill. Instead, it is human sinfulness that has enacted deadly structures of power. And if humans have lived with grace and hope and love, the credit belongs solely to the God who inspired them.

Of course, this does not mean that the biblical texts are innocent, mute bystanders if we harm others in light of their purported teachings. The Bible is as human as we are even as it is true that the Bible is breathed by God as much as God has breathed life into our bodies.

Yours is a heavy task as a reader of Scripture. Before you crack the spine of these ancient books, you already know that you will encounter God's holy word. But you also know that how you receive that word might bring life or it might bring death. In fact, we are probably safe to assume that what we read will in some way run contrary to God's hopes for the world. And yet we read nonetheless, trusting that even in the midst of our foibles and crimes, God's voice will resonate most clearly.

Recommended Reading

Blount, Brian K. *Cultural Interpretation: Reorienting New Testament Criticism.* Minneapolis, MN: Augsburg Fortress, 1995.

Brown, William P., ed. *Engaging Biblical Authority: Perspectives on the Bible as Scripture.* Louisville, KY: Westminster John Knox, 2007.

Carey, Greg. *Sinners: Jesus and His Earliest Followers.* Waco, TX: Baylor University Press, 2009.

Clark-Soles, Jamie. *Engaging the Word: The New Testament and the Christian Believer.* Louisville, KY: Westminster John Knox, 2010.

Dube, Musa. *Postcolonial Feminist Interpretation of the Bible.* St. Louis, MO: Chalice, 2000.

Ekbald, Bob. *Reading the Bible with the Damned.* Minneapolis, MN: Fortress Press, 2005.

Fretheim, Terence E. *God and World in the Old Testament: A Relational Theology of Creation.* Nashville, TN: Abingdon, 2005.

———. *What Kind of God? Collected Essays of Terence E. Fretheim.* Winona Lake, IN: Eisenbrauns, 2015.

González, Justo L. *The Story Luke Tells: Luke's Unique Witness to the Gospels.* Grand Rapids, MI: Eerdmans, 2015.

Jasper, David. *A Short Introduction to Hermeneutics.* Louisville, KY: Westminster John Knox, 2004.

Johnson, Luke Timothy. *Scripture and Discernment: Decision Making in the Church.* Nashville, TN: Abingdon, 1996.

Junior, Nyasha. *An Introduction to Womanist Biblical Interpretation*. Louisville, KY: Westminster John Knox, 2015.

Law, Timothy Michael. *When God Spoke Greek: The Septuagint and the Making of the Christian Bible*. Oxford, UK: Oxford University Press, 2013.

Metzger, Bruce M. *The Canon of the New Testament: Its Origin, Development, and Significance*. Oxford, UK: Oxford University Press, 1997.

Meyers, Carol. *Rediscovering Eve: Ancient Israelite Women in Context*. New York: Oxford University Press, 2013.

Newsom, Carol A., Sharon H. Ringe, and Jacqueline E. Lapsley, eds. *Women's Bible Commentary*. 3rd ed. Louisville, KY: Westminster John Knox, 2012.

Perkins, Pheme. *Introduction to the Synoptic Gospels*. Grand Rapids, MI: Eerdmans, 2009.

Segovia, Fernando F., and Mary Ann Tolbert. *Reading from This Place, Volume 1: Social Location and Biblical Interpretation in the United States*. Minneapolis, MN: Fortress Press, 1995.

———. *Reading from This Place, Volume 2: Social Location and Biblical Interpretation in Global Perspective*. Minneapolis, MN: Fortress Press, 2000.

Sharp, Carolyn J. *Wrestling the Word: The Hebrew Scriptures and the Christian Believer*. Louisville, KY: Westminster John Knox, 2010.

Appendix: Revised Gottwald Inventory

Instructions

The following "inventory" is a reflective exercise that helps readers determine how historical, environmental, and communal factors influence their interpretations of the Bible.[1] This inventory makes the assumption that, as readers, we *never read texts from nowhere*. We always bring all of ourselves to the task of reading. There is no sterile laboratory in which we can slough off the influences of the world and enter into "innocent" or value-free interpretation. We are in the world, and there is no escape.

But none of this is bad news! Our own history, identity, and context—our positionality—help us see things in the text that others don't. Recognizing how our positionality affects interpretation tunes our ears to how the Spirit might be speaking through the positionality of others, whose sojourn through the world shapes their reading of the Bible in profoundly different ways. Finally and most importantly, with the Spirit's help, this critical awareness will result in humility before God, the neighbor, and the text. Because we read from a finite place in history, our interpretations remain contingent, anchored in the particularities of our own history and situation.

The great Jewish scholar Michael Fishbane makes a similar point with characteristic eloquence:

"Interpretations come and go," said Martin Buber, "but the text remains throughout." And yet we must equally stress that the text remains precisely because of the comings and goings of interpretation. It is for this reason that everything depends on how we read; on how we enter the magic circle of a text's meanings; on how we smuggle ourselves into its words, and allow the texture of a text to weave its web around us.[2]

The act of "smuggling" ourselves into a text is not a voluntary exercise, not an interpretive option. It is an inevitability. Of chief importance is the recognition of this inevitability and the subsequent realization that we are never finally able to leave the magic circle. When God addresses us through these texts, we are always and at all times addressed from within place and time.

We recommend that you respond to these questions over several days. Try to resist the tendency to edit yourself too carefully. Write freely, without attention to grammar, punctuation, and so on. What's most important is that you write *honestly*.

1. Religious Communities

Have you ever been involved in religious communities? How would you describe those communities? Were they churches? Synagogues? Other types of religious communities? Did that/those communities have any connections to broader institutions (e.g., denominations, faith coalitions)? How did your experiences with these communities shape your interpretation or perception of the Bible?

2. Authoritative Criteria

How would you describe the Bible's status in the religious communities discussed in the previous question? Were there other acknowledged or unacknowledged sources of authority (e.g., confessions, writings, leaders, customs, personal experience, or social commitments)? Other possibilities?

3. Working and Formal Theology

Is the Bible important for your theology? If so, what role does it play? How has your understanding of the Bible changed over your lifetime? How does it differ from views advocated by religious communities you have participated in?

Is your working theology more or less the same as your formal theology, such as you might state in an application to a seminary or before a religious body?

4. Reading Practices

Where, when, and how often do you interact with the Bible? How do these practices affect your interpretation of Scripture?

5. Ethnicity and Culture

How do your ethnicity, culture, and consciousness influence your interpretation of the Bible? How does your family upbringing affect how you interpret and understand the Bible?

6. Upbringing

What was the characteristic view of the Bible in your childhood home? Have you stayed in continuity with that view? Do you now see the Bible rather differently than your parents did (or do)? If there have been major changes in your view of the Bible, how did these come about? How do you feel about differences in biblical understanding within your current family setting?

7. Gender and Sexual Identity

How does your gender and/or sexual identity influence your understanding and interpretation of the Bible?

8. Socioeconomic Class

How does your socioeconomic class influence your interpretation of the Bible? It may take considerable effort on your part to identify your class location. For starters, you can ask about work experience, inherited wealth, income, education, types of reading, news sources consulted, social and career aspirations, and so on, and you can ask these questions about yourself, your parents, your grandparents, your associates, your neighborhood, and your church.

9. Education

How does your level and type of education influence your interpretation of the Bible? If you have had technical or professional training in non-religious fields, how does this impact your way of reading the Bible?

10. Age

How does your age affect your interpretation of the Bible?

11. Political Position

How do your political positions influence your biblical interpretation? The term *political position* in this question refers to more than political party affiliation or location on a left-right political spectrum. It also takes into account how much impact one feels from society and government on one's own life and how much responsibility one takes for society and government, and in what concrete ways. Also involved is how one's immediate community/church is oriented toward sociopolitical awareness or how one's faith informs a particular political orientation.

12. Attitude toward Judaism

What is your view of the relationship between Judaism and Christianity? To what extent is your view informed by direct experience of Jews or Jewish communities? How does your view affect your understanding of the relationship between the Old and New Testaments and your understanding of the religious identity of Jesus, Paul, and other central figures in the New Testament?

13. Attitude toward Other Religions

What is your view of the relationship between Christianity and other world religions? To what extent is your view informed by direct experience of people from other religions? How do your views on other world religions affect how you read the Bible?

14. The Bible in Practice

Reflecting back on your experiences with the Bible, what are some of the dominant ways in which it was used? Such uses may include worship, preaching, church-school instruction, private study, Bible school training, ethical and theological resourcing, solitary or group devotions or spiritual exercises, and so on. How does the mix of uses of the Bible to which you have been or are currently exposed influence your biblical interpretation?

15. Bible Translation

How do the Bible translations and study Bibles you use influence your interpretation of the Bible? What translation(s) do you regularly or frequently use, and why?

16. Published Resources

Apart from Bible translations, do you use other published materials (e.g., study Bible notes, commentaries, books, blogs/vlogs, sermons) to help you interpret the Bible? Do these resources tend to communicate multiple points of view or a more-or-less single point of view? Do you accept these resources' interpretations without question, or do you feel free to disagree and consult other resources?

17. Intent and Effect of Biblical Preaching

How do your church and pastor (or you as pastor) understand the role of the Bible in preaching as an aspect of the mission of the church, and how does that understanding influence your own pattern of biblical interpretation?

18. Orientation to Biblical Scholarship

Are the categories and terminology of biblical scholarship completely new to you, or do you have some familiarity with them? How does your attitude toward and use or nonuse of biblical scholarship influence your biblical interpretation? Do you view scholarship positively or with suspicion? Does the biblical scholarship you are familiar with increase or decrease your sense of competence and satisfaction in Bible study?

19. Life Crises and/or Significant Events

Have you experienced crises in your life that led you into a different understanding of the Bible? If so, what has been the lasting effect of the crisis on your interpretation of the Bible?

20. Spirituality or Divine Guidance

What has been your experience of the role of the Bible in spiritual awareness or guidance from God? What biblical language and images play a part in your spiritual awareness and practice? How do you relate this "spiritual" use of the Bible to other ways of reading and interpreting the Bible? Do these different approaches to the Bible combine comfortably for you, or are they in tension or even open conflict?

◉➝◉ Notes

1. This inventory is modified from Norman K. Gottwald, "Framing Biblical Interpretation at New York Theological Seminary: A Student Self-Inventory on Biblical Hermeneutics," *Reading from This Place: Social Location and Biblical Interpretation in the United States* (Minneapolis, MN: Augsburg Fortress, 1995), 251–62.

2. Michael Fishbane, *Biblical Text and Texture: A Literary Reading of Selected Texts* (Oxford, UK: Oneworld, 1998), 141.